# *The Broke Diaries*

$$$$$$$$$$$$$$$$$$$$$$

## *The Completely True and Hilarious Misadventures of a Good Girl Gone Broke*

## *ANGELA NISSEL*

*VILLARD*
*NEW YORK*

VILLARD BOOKS is a registered trademark of Random House, Inc.
Colophon is a trademark of Random House, Inc.

Library of Congress Cataloging-in-Publication Data

Nissel, Angela.
The broke diaries: the completely true and hilarious misadventures
of a good girl gone broke/Angela Nissel.
        p.     cm.
ISBN 0-679-78357-1
1. Nissel, Angela.   2. College students—United States—Biography.
3. College students—United States—Finance, Personal.   I. Title.
LA229 .N55 2001
382.1'98—dc21      00-047321

Villard website address: www.villard.com
Printed in the United States of America on acid-free paper

987

*The Broke Diaries*

*Dedicated to my mother*
*and her sense of humor*

# Author's Note

The characters in this book are real, but it bears mentioning that I have used pseudonyms for a number of them in order to protect their privacy, and in a few cases I have gone a step further by altering their descriptions just to cover my ass even more. Though this is a work of nonfiction, I have taken certain storytelling liberties, particularly having to do with the timing of events. Where the narrative strays from strict nonfiction, my intention has been to remain faithful to the characters and to the essential drift of events as they really happened.

"You're a damn liar, Ang! This can't all be true. No one would date a lunatic chicken farmer just to get free rotisserie."

Well, I did. When you're as broke as I was, you really don't mind deranged people as long as they bring food.

Hmm, I guess some people would consider me deranged, too. What healthy person keeps a diary of the scandalous things she does to make ends meet?

Thing is, everyone has a broke diary. Maybe you never wrote yours down, perhaps your broke diary is just a collection of memories from college, or all those low-paying jobs you had. Maybe your broke diary is no memory, 'cause you're broke as hell right now and sitting in that bookstore chair planning on reading my whole book over a latte and a scone instead of buying it.

Yeah, I know how you feel. Yep, people used to say the "you're going to look back at these broke times and laugh one day" line to me, too. Thing was, I needed to laugh *while* I was broke, not later—when my checks were so rubber, I had to get them rotated and balanced. To facilitate the laughter, I started posting a few of my broke diary entries on the Web. Broke people the world over took a break from slurping up their ramen noodles to laugh at me. Seems even the brokest of the broke thought my fiscal dilemmas were a bit bizarre. (You mean everyone doesn't break up her landlord's marriage just to get out of paying rent? People have no creativity!)

Thankfully, those days of giving free laughs and lessons to

my fellow broke man are over. Some big powerful book publishing people surfed across my diary and now I'm getting paid
to write about being broke! Well, provided that you get up from
that bookstore chair and actually buy the book . . . or in a couple of years you'll be not buying the sequel to this book.

And I'll be eating more of Farmer Boy's pets. (It was a damn
tasty meal, though.)

*Two piece and a biscuit,*
*Ang*

*The Broke Diaries*

$$$$$$$$$$$$$$$$

Dear Broke Diary:

Knowledge should be free.

And today, at the University of Pennsylvania, it was.

Only with the truly broke can a beautifully planned day of study turn into a burglary.

I love having the same classes as my friends. Usually, when we combine our purchasing power, we can afford all of the books for the class. One set that we all share, of course.

But not this anthropology class me and Janelle, my closest brokest friend, are enrolled in. This class has three required books *and* a bulkpack (a bound collection of essays from multiple authors). What the hell was this professor thinking?

I wish they bootlegged books like they bootleg albums. Where's the man with the briefcase full of stolen books?

Eff a fake Gucci watch. Start hawking photocopies of textbooks. You'll be a tax-free millionaire in no time.

No, know what I want? Thugs who just rough up professors who assign too many books. Especially professors who assign books they themselves authored. The book thugs wouldn't hurt 'em, just, like, corner them in a lab late one night and scare them into shame.

> Thug [knocking petri dish to the floor]: Yeah, I knocked over your little dish! You wanna do something about it?! Huh, do you??!

Professor [cowering in corner]: Please, sir!!! Leave me be!! Is it money you're after? I don't have any money in here! Just fetal pigs!

Thug: Sure, you don't have any money! We know you're getting kickbacks from the publishing companies for assigning these overpriced books!! And how are you going to assign a book you wrote your damn self?!! Why, I should—

Professor: Please, take all the drugs you want! In fact, I'll make you some drugs! Please, go!

Thug [punches hole in Periodic Table of Elements Chart]: I'll be back.

Oops. I didn't mean to start writing a screenplay. Sorry. Just get a little emotional sometimes. Got all this aggression up in me 'cause, man, I wanna learn, too!

Anyway. Me and 'Nelle did split the cost of the anthro bulk-pack but, man, we were jonesing for that textbook. Not having that textbook has put us mad behind.

Yesterday, we made a plan to bridge that broke learning gap. Janelle is convinced Joel, the teaching assistant, gives her special looks during class. (Yes, she said "special looks." How funny, right?!! What the hell is a "special look"?) So she suggested we go to his office hours and double-team him: I'd kiss up and she'd flirt.

Anyway, I was down for the plan, but the only special look I want from Joel is the look he gives my midterms and final when he smacks an A on both of 'em.

Today was supposed to be the first day on the quest to have Joel smack my A.

Janelle and I met up in front of Van Pelt Library and walked over to the university museum. Just two normal, innocent college girls walking to class. We could have made the "Guide for Prospective Parents" video. Janelle even had a bow in her hair. Ah, it was perfect.

We were still pure and innocent as we walked up the museum stairs, down the left-end hall, and into Joel's office. He wasn't there, so we just plopped down on the beat-up office love seat and started chatting.

That's when we saw it. Perched on top of a stack of papers on his desk.

Yes, it was . . . The Textbook.

Okay, actually, 'Nelle saw it first. We were talking, and all of a sudden her eyes got wide like saucers. Her voice dropped to an urgent whisper. "Oh shit, Ang! Look! Look! On the desk!"

Mmmm, yes. That book looked beautiful in all of its unbroken-spined glory. Shiny, happy book. With the words "Educator's Edition" emblazoned in gold across the front. Polished gold, not dull gold like the cafeteria workers' teeth.

I wanted to pick it up, to touch it, to write down some of the sacred "Educator's Edition" notes I knew were contained therein.

I wanted to look in it so badly, but that's rude, right? You can't touch someone's stuff while they aren't there. Oh, but it was calling me. . . . It was so shiny, so new . . . so—

WOW.

Janelle's a bad sis.

I was scared to touch the book, but in some wild fit of broke bibliomania, her ass done picked it up and ran out the door with it.

Damn!

Ladies and gentlemen, the book has left the building!

I was thinking, Oh my God! Do I sit here? Do I follow her?

One of those lectures my mom gave me when I was little came into my head. How if my friends stole Now and Laters from the corner store and I was with them, I'd go to jail, too.

I can see us now, getting kicked out of college for this. Liberal politicians would use our dilemma as evidence of how unequal educational opportunities are: "They got kicked out of school for wanting to learn!"

And can you imagine me telling my mom what I got kicked out of school for?

Oh my God, what do I do?

Then reality kicked in.

Um, do I want to be the only one sitting here when Joel comes back and sees his book is missing?

I gotta have my girl's back. And I have to pass this class.

Viva la Stolen Textbook!

And an Educator's Edition, at that. Damn, I am so proud of Janelle. That's my girl!

Now that I'm home, and I realize we're probably not going to get caught, I'm a little jealous she has the textbook.

I'm going to go to the other T.A.'s office hours tomorrow. Bet he got an Educator's Edition book, too. I'll be damned if Janelle gets better grades *and* special looks.

*Misdemeanor,*

*Ang*

---

## OCTOBER 14

Dear Broke Diary:

I buy cat litter and get $1.21 change from my last $5 bill. I mean, there's nothing worse than being broke and having a studio apartment that smells like dirty cat litter, so I had to spend money on that, you know?

I make myself pancakes for breakfast. And lunch. For dinner a dear friend buys me McNuggets. No fries. (Hey, he's broke, too!)

I have no clean clothes, so I wash out an outfit by hand.

I have no conditioner, so I use mayonnaise.

*Poorly,*

*Ang*

---

## OCTOBER 15

Dear Broke Diary:

I have just enough batter left for two more pancakes. That's brunch.

I call my McNugget friend and break into tears. Life is hard, we both agree. He brings me chicken he cooked. I find a box of Rice-A-Roni way back in my kitchen cabinet that expired over a month ago. I figure it's still good, they just date it a month early so they don't get hit with lawsuits. I eat it.

It's good.

*San Francisco treatin',*

*Ang*

---

## OCTOBER 16

Dear Broke Diary:

I interview a deejay friend for a new magazine run by a class-mate. My deejay friend is paid, but he doesn't always like to share. I used to cook for him all the time. Picked him up from work at 3:00 and 4:00 A.M. He lends me $20 because he remembers all my sacrifices.

Then I get a baby-sitting gig! Quick $20 and food!

Problem: My car won't go over twenty miles per hour. Transmission is gone. It's eight years old, and has almost 150,000 miles on it, so what do I expect? Yes, I bought it used. I take the highway, going twenty mph with my blinkers on so I can get this baby-sitting loot on!

*Stop honking,*

*Ang*

---

## OCTOBER 20

Dear Broke Diary:

You see I haven't written an entry in four days. Because I had $40 in my pocket!!! I've never felt so rich in my life. I spent an entire day contemplating what I could do with my $40. Let's see, I could rent a car from Rent-A-Wreck, I could see the same movie seven times, I could buy three new CDs, or I could stop daydreaming and get some damn groceries.

I did just that! I made jerk chicken, even bought my cat a can of wet food to celebrate. Most of the stuff I bought was on sale, so yes, I am being smart with my wealth. (C'mon, it's $40, not a mutual fund.) I'm almost back to broke status now . . . so here's what I'm doing to save money:

Found out used-record stores will buy albums even if they say "Promo Copy: Not for Sale" in blinking red lights on the front.

Brushed my teeth with baking soda. (Don't think I'm gross, they're clean!)

Went jogging. It takes your mind off of problems.

Took a nice long bath. Nothing like a bubble bath to make you feel rich.

Placed a personal ad in the paper. Hey, it's one of the few things you can do for free. Plus, I'll probably get some free dinners out of it!

SF ISO *money,*

*Ang*

---

OCTOBER 21

Dear Broke Diary:

This senior-citizen guy who lives in my building says he hasn't been smelling my good cooking lately. I tell him how broke I am. He looks over the top of his glasses and sees my sad, emaciated eyes staring back at him. He begins reaching for his wallet. I object, but he insists. He pulls out some purple money. I'm thinking it's, like, a Jamaican dollar bill or something . . . but it's a damn food stamp! No joke, y'all. Old brother gave a sister a food stamp.

As wild as that was, you know I wasn't letting this five-dollar food stamp go to waste.

Plus, old man schools me that if I spend $4.01, I get ninety-nine cents in real money back!!!

Man, I spend like an hour in Thriftway (our neighborhood supermarket) trying to manipulate my purchase total so it'll be $4.01 exactly. I finally get to the front of the long-ass line, but when I go to give the cashier my stamp of life, she starts frowning.

"You know I can't accept that without a booklet."

"Booklet?" I'm thinking sis wants a bible tract or something. I am all confused until this little blond-haired lady behind me whips out a "booklet" from her back pocket and holds it in the air.

"Theees! Theees ez uh booook-lett!" Damn, a person not from the United States had to school me on what a government food stamp booklet was.

I put my head down and start walking out of the store really quickly. I hear in the wind as I am crossing the automatic door threshold, "Food stamp void on register six!"

Damn.

Hungry,

Ang

OCTOBER 26

Dear Broke Diary:

Well, I've been cooling out studying for a few days straight, so I'm really not too concerned with money right now.

I did have to wash some clothes today. My five-story apartment building houses about sixty apartments. All sixty apartments share a nice little basement laundry room. Two washers. Two dryers. Two families of roaches. This is like a luxury building. Janelle's building only has a tin washboard.

I take the manual elevator downstairs to wash my clothes. I have $1.30. One nickel and five quarters. So what if I need six quarters to wash and dry? I will make the machine believe my nickel is a quarter.

The guy who designed the change slot probably didn't go to an Ivy League school and I do, so I'm smarter than him. When I'm broke, I get conceited; it's the only thing that gets me through. (Okay, so I'm also not thinking that the girl who goes to Penn has only $1.30 and the person who designed this coin slot is probably upper-middle-class.)

I drop my clothes into the washer and proceed to put two quarters and a nickel into the slots. I bet this machine won't know the difference between a quarter and a nickel!

Wrong! I'm thinking it knows my nickel isn't a quarter because the nickel doesn't stand up as tall as the quarter, so I put tape on the bottom of the nickel to make it the same height as the quarters. Still no go.

I try jerking the coin slot back and forth at the speed of light, assuming that the machine will get confused or feel sorry for my broke ass and just take the damn nickel.

So anyway, I got a nice upper-arm workout, but in the end I had to use three quarters for the washing machine. I let my stuff drip-dry once it was done.

Besides the drip-dry, today wasn't a bad day. I got a free sample of Secret deodorant from this beauty salon on campus. I can smell a free sample even when I have a sinus cold.

*Ang*

---

## NOVEMBER 1

Dear Broke Diary:

My broke life is getting weirder and weirder. Today was the craziest day.

I got paid from my little part-time job yesterday. When I woke up this morning, I realized I needed to buy a new broom. Mine has about ten bristles left. They keep getting snagged on my carpet. I know you're not supposed to sweep a carpet, and I feel like a nut even when I'm doing it, but vacuum cleaners cost more than my sofa did. Even if I *could* afford a vacuum cleaner, it'd be a waste to buy one for an apartment the size of a holding cell.

So, I went to Wal-Mart today to get my broom.

And I can never go back.

I got banned from Wal-Mart. And it wasn't even my fault. Hmm . . . maybe it was my fault on some level. I should have known a Saturday morning is the wrong time to go to Wal-Mart. I usually go on my class-free Friday afternoons, and that's bad enough. Last Friday I saw a customer hurl Kodak film at a cashier's head over a pricing dispute, so I should have known that Saturdays would be even worse.

So, I'm chilling with the weekend Wal-Mart crowd and when I'm done picking out my needed items (a binder, some shampoo, and my broom), I head to the checkout area.

Is anyone else a slow-line magnet or is that my own personal birth defect? Why do the people in front of me always want to argue over a price? The lady in front of me is insisting that the rubber bands are on sale. "Get a manager if you don't believe me. The sign in front of the rubber bands said they were a dollar!"

After about six minutes of rubber ranting, I notice that the cashier at the next register is counting her drawer and has no customers. I walk three steps to the left, lean over into her aisle, and ask if she's open. She replies that she is not, she is waiting for some change; so I backtrack the three steps and regain my place next to my cart. Finally the woman in front of me gets her bag o' bands for the correct price and I start placing my purchases-to-be on the counter.

Hot, angry words erupt behind me:

"No! No! No!! Oh no you don't! Get to the rear of the line!"

The words land right on the back of my neck, slide down my shirt, and flick on my adrenaline button. I *know* this chick behind me is not yelling at me. Lord, let me turn around calmly and see who she is and if she is indeed screaming at the back of *my* neck.

My calmness and I, we turn around to face the source of the screamed words but are blinded temporarily as the woman who just shouted *pushes into us* and slams her Cottonelle on the counter.

"I'm going next!" Toilet Paper Lady bellows.

Okay, Ang, hold on to calmness and just protest her pushing in a sweet, serene manner.

"Excuse me, but I am next."

"Honey, you moved, you lose!" she snorts, and keeps shoving items onto the counter.

*You moved, you lose?* The last time I heard that line I was telling Johnny he couldn't cut back in the dessert line after he left to get Tater Tots. Then we had our afternoon nap.

There is no teacher here today, so I can't get Toilet Paper Lady's recess privileges taken away. I'll just continue the "counter meanness with kindness" approach.

I try unsuccessfully to explain to Toilet Paper Lady that I was simply inquiring about the status of the other register so we could *all* get out of here faster. From my numerous checkout-line experiences, I know that "moving" consists of moving your cart as well as your body. I had simply taken three baby steps to ask the other cashier if she was open, therefore my spot in line was reserved.

"So, as you see, technically I did not change lines. I rest my case."

"What are you talking about? Shut up!" She spurts this objection while forcefully pushing past me to place her toiletries on the counter.

Now I'm pissed. I completely stop and stare her dead in the face. I can feel sweat forming along my hairline. If I have to fight, God, and it has to be in a Wal-Mart, then let's make this a good one. Let's get ready to rumble, baby, 'cause if she pushes me one more time, I'm going to grab this three-ring binder from my cart and pitch it at her left eye.

In the midst of planning my attack, I swear one of those ubiquitous yellow Wal-Mart smiley faces started whispering in my ear like one of those wise old karate masters from badly dubbed martial-arts movies. "Pick your battles wisely, young broke Angie. Wal-Mart battle not worth it. Let the bitch go."

What influential power this smiley face has. I turn to the woman, smile, and say, "If it's that important that you go next, go ahead. If that makes you happy, go right ahead. It's not worth it."

She sucks her teeth and shouts, "Yeah, it *would* make me happy! Excuse me!" She pushes into me again.

Okay, all this bumping-into-me shit has got to stop. I want to hit her with something! Where's the nunchaku aisle, Smiley Face? I tried to be nice! I really did! I even smiled at her! Who else smiles in the midst of battle? My eye is twitching, my fingers are curling into a ball, and I really, really need to sock the shit out of her! Please have my back, Smiley Face!

Wise Smiley drops down from the ceiling. "Young broke Angie, her pushing behavior not acceptable. . . . You may now FIGHT!"

Thank you!!!

Okay, I just have to let her make the first move. She's in Wal-Mart because she's broke. Broke people love lawsuits.

If she makes the first move, she can't sue me for my future earnings.

I'm still staring her right in the eye. Slowly I say, "You know what? I was going to let you go, but you keep purposely bumping into me. I'm tired of people like you who don't have anything better to do than to cause trouble and make everyone miserable. I'm going next."

I must have been louder than I thought because I see the cashier reach cautiously for the phone above her register. She doesn't dial, though. She looks like she is torn between the excitement of the pending fight and concern for her safety. I also see that other customers have stopped dead in their tracks to look at the outcome of the "battle of the line space."

Oh well, I've stated my intentions, so I start readying my items for checkout. As I lean in to grab items from my cart, I feel the biggest push yet; it nearly folds me over the damn cart!

When I turn around to confront her, she shifts her weight as if she is going to strike me. I kick at the bottom rack of my shopping cart so the steering bar will hit her in the belly. I hope it will knock her back a few feet, but it barely moves her. She's no average-size woman. She lurches forward with her fingers separated like she is going to grab my hair. I back up and grab the broom from my cart by the bristle end and just start swinging it like I am out of my damn mind. My mom always says to act like you're totally insane if you are ever about to get robbed, 'cause that scares most people more than a gun. I hope it works in this situation.

Well, I must look like the National Alliance for the Mentally Ill poster girl, because she actually takes a few steps backwards. She just backs up, breathing heavy and looking at me.

My body temperature would crack a thermometer right now. I just want someone to hold her down so I can repeatedly whack her in the head with the broomstick until she apologizes for pushing me. Adrenaline is a bitch, boy. I'm not a violent person, but I'm so pissed I think I should go for it. I shouldn't back down now!

Then I see a little blond kid with a juice stain on his shirt pointing at me in amazement. His eyes are so big. He is just so mesmerized by our fight. I feel so bad. Damn kids. I swear, if I put this broomstick down because I feel bad that this kid has to see a fight, his parents better not let him watch wrestling or play violent video games. Only wholesome cartoons.

Luckily some guy (he might have been with Toilet Paper Lady, I'm not sure) rushes over and grabs her, so I lower my cleaning weapon just a little bit. My broomstick of doom is still ready if he lets her go, though.

A male manager arrives soon after that guy and screams at me to "put the fucking broom down." He then inquires as to what our "damn problems" are. She tells him that I tried to cut in line, but amazingly the cashier sticks up for me. The manager tells Toilet Paper Lady to follow him to get checked out at the jewelry counter. I thank him. As Toilet Paper Lady is following him to the register, she looks back at me and mouths, "Bitch."

Yes, I'll be a bitch, but this bitch is checking out at this register. Now, go on ahead to jewelry. Go on, now.

My cashier apologizes to me as she's ringing me up. I tell her it wasn't her fault. I start to feel a little better, but I realize I might still see Toilet Paper Lady in the parking lot, so I don't let myself get too happy as I head towards the exit doors.

As I approach the doors, I see the manager standing there. I smile at him and am actually getting ready to thank him when he puts his hand on the edge of my cart to prevent it from moving.

"Young lady, I don't know what happened, but I told the other woman this and I will tell you the same: I don't want to see you in this store anymore."

What?? Oh no he didn't! Do I have to whip my broomstick out on him, too?

This has got to be one big joke. I start to argue my innocence, but I've had enough confrontation for the day.

I even look around to see if another wise yellow smiley face will pop up and give me some words of advice, but nada. Sensei Smiley has abandoned me.

Stuff like this doesn't happen in Saks Fifth Avenue. Ever.

You know what else? This Wal-Mart had loads of security cameras. I am sure I'll be reminded of this li'l skirmish later in life. If a camera was focused on the aisle we were in, that footage is going to be a favorite on the security-guard circuit. One day, I am going to have a normal job and some stranger is going to roll up on me screaming, "Oh my God! It's the Broom Girl from the Wal-Mart Underground series! I love your work!"

Anyway, like I said, I didn't argue my innocence. What's the point? I mean, what are they going to do? Post my photo on the door? Hire a doorman just to keep me away?

I'll be back.

I'll just wait a month.

*Exiled from rollback prices,*

*Angie*

---

## NOVEMBER 6

Dear Broke Diary:

Today was one of the saddest days of my broke life. One of those days you get mad at homeless people for assuming you have money to give them. Don't they have Internet access?

Don't they see I've been putting some of my Broke Diaries on the Web? Sheesh . . . the nerve . . .

Anyhow, I started the day by gathering all of my loose nickels together. I even found a quarter in my bathroom. It was a bicentennial quarter, so I tried to convince the guy who sells sodas near the school museum that it was really worth fifty cents. Strangely, people don't think I'm funny when I'm trying to con them. He didn't take my fifty-cent quarter, so I popped it into a vending machine along with four nickels and had a Rice Krispies Treat and some water for breakfast.

Oh, let me get to the embarrassment. My stomach was growling by the time I headed home for dinner. I had 33 cents left in my pocket. Well, not actually in my pocket; I have a hole in my coat pocket, so the coins had fallen into the lining of my jacket. I have to hold my coat in the air vertically so all of the coins align themselves under the hole, then I shake them out. You probably think I'm joking, but I promise you, I am not.

Anyway, I remembered that the corner store Jenny's Vegetables or Peggy's Fruit (depending on which window you're looking into) sells Top Ramen for 35 cents a pack. I went in, headed straight to the ramen, and oh my goodness! The sign said 70 cents! Oh, whew, that's for the *real* Oriental noodles. The Top Ramen is 35 cents.

I was sooooooo embarrassed. I only had 33 cents. I (please don't laugh) put the money on the counter and quickly attempted to dash out the door with my chicken-flavored salt noodles. The store guy called me back! I looked up instinctively. I should have run! Why didn't I just run???!! He told me the noodles are 35 cents. I tried to sound sincere with my apology. I told him I thought the sign said 33 cents yesterday, so that's all I brought with me. Could he wait while I run home and get the two cents? I showed him my student I.D. to let him know I was not a thief.

He shook his head and motioned for me to either "get the hell out of his store and *never* come back" or "get the money and *do* come back." I don't know. He said something like "Nyeh" and swiped his hand in my direction.

I can't translate hand motions well. And I didn't have two more cents, so I didn't go back.

The noodles: tasty!!!

MSG,

ANG

---

## NOVEMBER 8

Dear Broke Diary:

It's still too soon for me to go back to Wal-Mart. My phone died on me, so I had to go to Kmart ("mart" must mean "cheap" in some other language or something, huh?) on payday to buy a new one.

Back at Kmart the next day because the phone's push buttons didn't work. Exchange nonworking phone for the same $9.99 model.

No dial tone on the second phone. Remarkably, I *did* pay this month's phone bill, so I know it's the phone.

Back at Kmart customer service once again to return that second phone. I am told to go get the same model phone off the shelf and bring it back to customer service. This time, while I'm back in the electronics department, I open the box up to make sure all of the phone's parts are there, at least.

A mart girl scolds me.

"Sorry, miss. You can't open the phone boxes."

"Look, this is my third time buying this phone. I just want to make sure all of the pieces are here."

"Oh. I understand. Maybe you should get a different phone. That one is really cheap."

No duh! That's why I'm buying it. Because it's cheap it shouldn't *work*? Take it off the damn shelf, then!!!

Do you think I *want* to have the bright blue phone with the curly cord while everyone else has high-megahertz cordless phones they can walk to the store with?

*But thanks for the suggestion,*

*Ang*

---

NOVEMBER 10

Dear Broke Diary:

I woke up soooo hungry this morning.

Checked my fridge for potential nourishment. I only had two expired eggs on the bottom shelf and some old-ass Hi-C and barbecue sauce congregating together on the upper level.

On to the cabinets: a tube of grits. (Why are grits and oats the only foods that come in tubes?) I peer into the eyes of the Quaker Oats guy gracing the label. I meditate. . . . I feel like Pavlov's dog. My mouth is just a-watering.

Please-let-there-be-enough-for-one-serving-of-grits-please-let-there-be-enough-for-one-serving-of-grits. I chant this in my head like a sacred mantra.

I open the tube top and peer in.

A grit stares back at me.

Hel-lo? Did y'all hear me? One grit. A grit. Una gritora.

GRIT
(10x M₉)

I have never seen a solitary grit in my life. Why did I stick a tube of grits back in the cabinet with only one grit left?

I look in the other cabinet behind the NyQuil, the aspirin, the Theraflu, and the prescription pill bottles dating back to 1987, and I locate another tube of grits. I'm tripping out. I do the Gritfest dance.

Grit directions: For a single serving, boil one cup of water and add three tablespoons of grits.

Cool, I definitely have three tablespoons here.

I throw mad pepper on my grits to make up for my lack of butter. I put the bowl down on the floor (I have no table, my brother borrowed it and never gave it back) and sit on the bed, getting ready to chow down. Phone rings, so I get back up to get it.

It's a close relative (gotta protect people's privacy, so let's call this person "CR" for short). She needs me to type up something for her. As I go to sit back down on the bed, I knock over my bowl o' pepper grits. I scream into the phone.

CR asks what the hell I'm doing.

"I just spilled the last little bit of food I have all over the floor! I can't believe it! I am so hungry, I have no food. My check doesn't clear until Monday and it's only for seventy-seven dollars! My grits, my grits, my grits, my grits . . ."

"I don't know what to tell you, baby. You're an adult now, go find some food."

Okay, CR, up against the wall. . . . Now slowly put the "Tough Love" book down.

Find some food?

Do I look like a damn hunter-gatherer? When's the last time you've seen bands of black women foraging the 'hood for berries?

Of course, I can't say this to CR. But dag, can I just get a little love for putting myself through college? Can a struggling sis get some turkey sausage or lactose-reduced milk?

My cat approaches. I know he feels my pain. He's come to comfort me. . . . No, he walks right by me. He licks at the gritty carpet. He walks by me again, he rubs up against me. He purrs. He goes back to licking the grits.

HOT BREAKFAST SCORE SHEET:
Cat with no job: 1
Broke chick: 0

Sigh,
Ang

---

NOVEMBER 12

Dear Broke Diary:

I saw a sign today. The sign said "All Pants $2."

The sign was hanging off of a rack of clothes outside of the local dry-cleaning place.

Well, guess what—I finally got my pants out of the dry cleaner today! They were on the $2 rack! They would have cost me $9 to get out the regular way! Woohoo! I missed my pants. They'd been in there three months! Always had something better to do with my $9, so I never could seem to get them out.

This is great! Just when I was seriously considering donating my eggs to a needy infertile couple, that sign was like a nudge telling me to keep my head up and slow my stroll to the stirrups.

Oh, be honest. Don't act like you haven't considered cashing in on your eggs or anything else on your body you have extra of. Bone marrow. Kidney. Eye. That's what they're there for, you know. Duh.

*Poached,*

*Angie*

---

NOVEMBER 17

Dear Broke Diary:

I need to contact the people who make No Frills stuff.

First, I gotta find out *where* they make No Frills items. Is there a No Frills plant, and if there is, would I be able to find it, since No Frills doesn't advertise? Is it just a white building where everything gets delivered in unmarked white trucks? Is it a brand name, or is it just, like . . . there? Why is No Frills so damn secretive? Don't the people who own No Frills want to get recognized for their hard work?

Okay, so I don't want to thank the No Frillers. I want to write a letter of complaint. 'Cause dammit, there are few things worse than losing money on a venture you thought would save you money.

Like this effin' No Frills mustard I bought.

You know that nasty yellowish water stuff that comes out the first few times you squeeze a mustard container? That water is always supposed to be followed by regular mustard, right? Yeah, that's what I thought, too.

Well, I bought this No Frills mustard and there was no creamy mustard afterflow. Just 100 percent pure-grade yellow mustard water. Every time I squeezed the damn thing, out came more mustard water.

The bottle clearly said "Mustard" (and that's all it said), so I'm squeezing the bottle for five straight minutes.

While I am applying the death grip to the bottle, I'm hoping there is some real mustard in it and it's just engaged in a battle with the mustard water but that soon my mustard will emerge victorious. This whole bottle can't be a waste.

Halfway through, I realize it is indeed a waste.

Where's the toll-free No Frills number? Other products have numbers on their packaging, where is the one for No Frills?

See, there's something strange going on here. . . .

Why does No Frills sometimes get a whole aisle in the supermarket to itself? Why is it usually not mixed in with the other stuff? Why does no one ask these questions? Why aren't any of the news shows doing investigative reports on No Frills?

Because no one cares about broke people.

Let French's or some other high-end mustard mess up and it would be all over the news.

Now I have to eat a dry sandwich. To top that off, I have to eat it with "end" bread. The bread at the end of the loaf. I never used to eat that when I was a kid. It seemed defective.

Now I'm eating a dry slice of end bread wrapped around two slices of turkey ham. I fold the turkey ham several times to make the sandwich seem thicker.

*My, times have changed,*

Ang

NOVEMBER 20

Dear Broke Diary:

No kid ever says, "I want to be a bill collector when I grow up!"

Well, I know if my future kids ever say that, I'll take them to a psychiatrist until they start saying "police officer" and "doctor" like the other first-graders.

I'm so tired of these people calling my house trying to act like they are my friends in an attempt to fool me into admitting I'm really me.

It's the same thing every time:

Bill Collector: Hi, can I speak to Angela?
Me [trying to sound mean]: Who dis?
Bill Collector: This is Gretchen.
Me: Angela is not here. [Click.]

I mean, c'mon now. I don't have any friends named Gretchen! Don't these bill collectors understand that women know the names of all their female friends? An unknown woman calling can't be good under any circumstances. If she's not trying to collect something, she's trying to sell something. If it's neither of those, she's found your number in her man's pocket. An unknown woman calling another woman's house is automatically going to make the callee put her guard up. Not a good way to start off a bill collection attempt.

*Gretchen.* Sheesh.

You know, if they'd be honest with me, I'd be honest with them. The conversation would go like this:

Bill Collector: Hi, this is Gretchen from Collections. . . .
Me: I don't have your money, Gretchen. [Click.]

See, we could save a whole two lines of conversation.

I'm sorry. I know I'm in motormouth mode, it's just that a bill collector had the nerve to call my house this morning about a bill that wasn't even mine. Just some bill they decided to pin on me.

"Give it to Angela, she won't notice one more."

Thing is, this is the third time she called this week. You don't call my house three times to ask for money that I don't really owe you.

I'm looking at the collection agency number on my caller I.D. and I'm getting madder with each ring. I don't want to have to curse this lady out. She's just doing her job. I'll just make this easy on both of us: What would she say if they think I'm dead?

I think it throws some unlucky vibes in the air to actually declare yourself deceased, so with a little mumbling and wordplay, I hope I got this misinformed billing department off of my back. Listen in and feel free to off yourself as well.

Me: Hello?
Gretchen: Hi, is Angela Nissel there?
Me: No, I'm sorry. She passed away intotheotherroom. May she rest in peace onthecouch.

Gretchen started stammering apologies. Then *she* hung up. Problem solved.

Well, I hope the problem is solved. And, um, if you don't see any more entries from me, that probably means I got struck by lightning or something, so um, maybe you shouldn't try this one until you check back and make sure I'm still alive and writing.

Buried underapileofbills,

Angie

---

NOVEMBER 22

Dear Broke Diary:

I went to New York to see my friend Mario last weekend. I had just enough money to take the New Jersey Transit train there. But, of course, he wasn't at the train station when I arrived, and I had *no* cash on me.

Okay, no cash and no friend. I needed to call him, so what could I do?

Ah, yes, the Visa debit card. One always has a few dollars on a debit card, because ATMs don't give out singles. I dunno about you, but even if I'm out of toilet paper, I will not walk up to a human teller and ask to take $2 out of an account that has $2.15 in it. That's just a little *too* embarrassing.

Anyway, I'm getting off track. I need to call Mario and I know I have about $6 in my bank account, which is, of course, connected to my Visa debit card. So I find a pay phone that accepts Visa and dial Mario's number. The call goes through, so I assume that I had enough money on the card to make the call. I hang up before the answering machine picks up so I won't get charged. (Well, I assume they didn't charge me. No answer, you usually get your coins back. Should be the same with a credit or debit card, right?)

Five more minutes go by and still no Mario, so I call again. This time I leave a message.

Ten more minutes and no damn Mario, so I call a third time and leave a really caustic message. (Which served no purpose except to make me feel better. If he's not there, he won't hear it! Duh!)

Mario, brother, you've really got me hopping mad. I don't like standing around the train station all alone. With my overnight bag, it's obvious I'm from out of town. I start remembering all those stupid after-school specials where the girl leaves town without telling her parents and some pimp named Sweets picks her up and smoothly convinces her that he is going to make her into a star. She's soon strung out on some corner, convinced that prostitution is the usual route towards getting a movie role.

Well, no Sweets wanna-be is going to eyeball me and think I'm lost in this city because I've been standing around this train station for a half hour looking alone and worried. I'm going to try to page Mario. I whip out the debit card again and enter the pay-phone number into his pager. While waiting for him to call back on that phone, I try calling his home phone one more time from the next phone over.

Still no answer. I'm really nervous. I try calling four other friends who have graduated and moved to NYC, but none of them are home.

I hate Mario! He sucks! I'm going to wait ten more minutes and then I'm going to figure out a way to get home.

Nine minutes and one more call to his house later, Mario finally shows up babbling some weak excuses. I give him the cold shoulder and decide to make him feel guilty for at least a couple of hours, but change my mind and leave my grudge on the N train so we can relax and have some fun. We end up having a ball. All the phone calls and his having me wait at the train station alone is pretty much forgotten.

Until today.

I got ten bounced-check notices in the mail.

*Ten.*

Each bounced check carries a $30 fee.

Three hundred dollars in bounced-check fees.

That's about four weeks' pay. One twelfth of my yearly income.

This has to be a mistake. I call the toll-free number on Bank M's bounced-check notices.

"No, there's no mistake, ma'am. You charged ten phone calls to your checking account, but you didn't have enough money to cover any of them."

I am almost in tears as I try to argue that since the calls were connected, I assumed that I had enough money. There was no notice on the phone of how much each call cost. I surely wouldn't have made *ten* calls if I didn't think I had enough money. I paid $300 for ten local calls? I am begging this woman to remove the overdraft charges. I can't afford to have a negative $300 account balance. Especially since I have direct deposit! This bank ain't sucking up my checks to pay for those calls!

"You don't have a negative account balance, ma'am."

I don't? Whew! Yeah! Now that's what I'm talking about! They've seen my side of the story!

"We already took the fees out of a seven-hundred-dollar check that was direct-deposited yesterday."

Did I say *almost* in tears? Scratch that. I started bawling after she said that.

"Please, ma'am. Tell me you're joking! That seven-hundred-dollar check was student-loan money! Please, this can't happen. Is there anyone I can speak to?" I'm stuttering and sucking in tears. Don't want to start bawling on the phone to a stranger, but this is much worse than I thought. If it was just a negative account, I could have stopped all of my direct deposits, closed my account, and just owed the bank $300 for the rest of my life.

No, this is much worse. That was rent and food money for this month! And it's a loan, so I'm paying interest on it! These ten local calls are going to end up costing me $400 after the interest kicks in, and hey, they just might get me evicted, since I can't pay my rent now!

The customer-service agent transfers me to a supervisor. Supervisor says she feels sorry for me, but there is nothing she can do. She suggests I go to my local branch and try to ask the manager to waive the charges. There is no guarantee that the charges will be removed, but she admits she has known it to happen in the past.

I bike over to the bank to do just that. While pedaling, I am giving myself a pep talk like I am the quarterback of the Broke Super Bowl.

"C'mon, Ang! You can do it! Go get your money back! Hike!"

The first customer-service rep I speak with is very nice, but of course she has to hand the matter over to her supervisor. Supervisor is a complete ass.

Talking to her is like talking to a wall. A mean graffiti-covered wall. Finally I just ask her to close my account.

She protests none. A little argument would be nice. I just gave your damn bank $300 for nothing! Don't you want to keep me as a customer?

Well, whatever. At least I know some landlord/tenant law. My landlord can't evict me right away. He has to get a court order or something first. While he's talking to the judge, somehow I will find a way to hustle up the rest of my rent money. I can always pawn my high school class ring again. I got $75 for it last time.

Supervisor hands me $387.90. The amount left in my account from the $700 student-loan check after they deducted their $300 bounced-check fee and the cost of the actual calls ($12.10).

There's nothing I can do about it now. I'll take my $387.90 elsewhere, and I *will* get my rent money somehow. All of this is just making me a better hustler. There's a lesson in everything.

The lesson in this is not to date tardy men.

I'm through with him and I'm through with this bank, too.

*I'll just be taking my business elsewhere!*

Angie

---

NOVEMBER 23

Dear Broke Diary:

I couldn't take my business elsewhere.

No one wants my business.

Fine. You know, I've gotten over the fact that my old bank basically stole $300 from me, but now i've got to accept that *every* bank in Philadelphia refuses even to touch my money?

Ever wonder why some people use check-cashing agencies? I used to think, Why don't they just go to the bank?

Well, maybe they're just like me: total financial-institution rejects.

Yes, I have just joined the ranks of check-cashing chicks the world over. I have nowhere else to go. No bank will deal with me.

Okay, I'll stop stalling and tell you. It's kinda embarrassing.

You know how yesterday I took the rest of my student-loan money out of that old bank?

Well, today I just figured I'd pop into another bank, fill out a few forms, and open a new checking account.

Yeah, sure.

When I left the house this morning to go to Bank F, I was proud and full of energy. I felt I had taught that evil old Bank M a lesson by closing my account. I voted with my dollars, yeah! And dammit, one day I am going to be middle-class, and they'll want me and my money back. (I now realize this was faulty thinking. The bank doesn't want middle-class. Middle-class usually bounces maybe one to two checks a year. I bounced ten in thirty minutes. I made them $300 in thirty minutes. If I were a stock, everyone would invest in me.)

I finally get to Bank F. I sign in and sit in the waiting area for over thirty minutes. Finally the only financial specialist (read: customer-service rep) working calls my name. All right! Let's do this!

I rise from the green seat. The financial specialist smiles at me and introduces herself as Ms. Williams.

Ms. Williams leads me back to her little utilitarian desk. There are papers all over it. I can see someone's name and Social Security number on one of them. God, I hope she doesn't leave my personal information lying around like that. I just saw a special news report on identity theft. Then again, what the hell would someone want to steal my identity for? I don't own anything, plus I have bad credit. They'd be one pissed-off identity thief.

So anyway, yo, Ms. Williams! I want to open an account.

"Well, great. I can help you with that. If you could just get two pieces of I.D. ready while I get some papers for you to fill out. Are you opening a checking or savings?"

I answer her query with a cheerful "Checking, please," while digging through my backpack for my driver's license and school I.D.

We both flash our pearly whites one more time before she sashays on back to get the forms.

I fill out the papers quickly and hand them over with my I.D. and initial deposit.

She has to go "in the back" once more (what's in the back?), so she hands me a pamphlet on certificates of deposit to read over while she's gone.

"Read this. For the future," she says.

Yes, for the future. Of course.

I crack open the pamphlet. She says she'll be back "in a minute."

She's gone for more than a minute, but hey, that's just more time for me to engross myself in future investment strategies.

In the middle of planning my third portfolio, I see two shadows creep across the desk. I look up. Someone is with Ms. Williams.

Oh, of course. The woman's tag reads "Supervisor."

What the hell did I do wrong this time?

Ms. Williams begins to answer my unspoken inquiry.

"I'm sorry, Ms. Nissel, but we can't open an account for you here. This is my first time dealing with someone with a ChexSystems record, so I brought out my supervisor to make sure I do everything correctly."

Okay, how exactly do you reject someone's money "correctly"? Is she to rip up my forms at a certain angle? Why'd she have to bring out the supervisor? Just tell me to get my broke ass up and leave.

But wait, hold up . . . what's this "ChexSystems" crap she said?

Supervisor speaks: "Ms. Nissel, did you have an account at Bank M?"

Damn, yeah, I did. So what's it to you? I'm leaving them to be with you! Don't worry about my past!

She actually doesn't want me to reply. If she did, she'd have paused after she posed that question to let me say something. She just lets out a sigh and keeps on talking.

Supervisor is saying Bank M "reported me" as having a "history of account mishandling or suspected fraud" and she can't open an account for me because I'm a "risk."

She slides my $387.90 across the desk to me.

I push it back to her.

I mean, what the hell? I was making a phone call!! I'm on a suspected fraud list because I didn't want to be stranded in a New York City train station??!! And Bank M got $300 for those phone calls! If there is any fraud in that, it ain't on my end!!

Grrr . . .

Ms. Williams pushes my money back towards me and lets out another sigh. I speak Sigh Language, and I know this is a "you're wasting my time" sigh.

"Ms. Nissel, you can open an account here when you get off of the ChexSystems list."

Here's this ChexSystems again. Who is Chex and how can I get out of his damn system?

"Ms. Nissel, you are welcome to open an account with us in five years, when your ChexSystems file is clear."

Five years! I might have kids by then. Won't my kids be embarrassed when all the other soccer moms go to the ATM and I'm going to the check-cashing joint? This is ridiculous. All this for some damn local phone calls to a guy I probably won't even remember in a couple of months?

I want BANK! I want an account! I'm not leaving here until I have an account. No, hold on. I'm not going to get upset. I'll just open a savings account instead, since they are so afraid of my past check-bouncing transgressions.

I smile.

"Okay, I'll just open a savings."

"No."

Damn, lady! What the eff?!! You can't bounce a savings account! C'mon, Supervisor Lady! Have a mind of your own! Screw ChexSystems! Please, please, please, *let me give you my money!!!*

Not that I'm not already embarrassed enough, right? Ms. Williams, who has been silent all this time, raises her hand and asks Supervisor, "Are there any banks where she would be allowed to open an account?"

Am I in a ChexSystems training classroom now? Is this a

question-and-answer session? I am her ChexSystems trainer now, I guess, huh? I should be getting paid for this. I'm outta here.

I grab my cash and leave.

I've done enough begging. I call two other banks when I get home and ask if they belong to the Cult of ChexSystems. They both do.

Turns out ChexSystems is a consumer reporting agency that collects information on delinquents like me and shares it among every bank in the U.S. Once a bank turns you in to Mr. Systems, you are pretty much relegated to a long period of check-cashing joints and money orders (aka "No bank for you! Next!").

My rent is way past due. Tomorrow I've gotta go to the check-cashing spot and get a money order.

You're coming with me, Broke Diary. I know this one will be fun.

I should have known better than to go to a bank whose initials are F.U.

*Eff Chex,*

*Ang*

---

**NOVEMBER 24**

Dear Broke Diary:

I am writing to you from inside one of the major poor portals: the Check-Cashing Joint.

Yep, that's right. I am really teetering on the edge of this temporarily broke/permanently poor dividing line because of this whole ChexSystems episode. All I need is one push from the left and I might trip over that line and land smack-dab on Poor.

I had to tell my boss to stop my direct deposit because, of course, deposit means "to place somewhere" and if you've been keeping up, you know my money has no place to go. Yep, I got homeless money. Me and my $77.12 paycheck are just looking for a cot and some hot cocoa until we get back on our feet and find a bank home again.

The Check-Cashing Joint is kinda like a homeless shelter for money. Well, a homeless shelter with a door charge. They know the only reason you're there is because you have nowhere else to go, but they take advantage of the situation by charging you fees for *everything*. First-time check-cashing fee. Payroll-check fee. Welfare-check fee. Breathing too hard while in line? Extra-breath fee. You can't just be sucking in all the check-cashing air for free! Pay up!

Think I'm exaggerating? Let's see how I fare with my $77.12 paycheck. How much of that $77.12 do you think I will get after they take out their fees?

Oh yeah, I gotta get a money order to pay my rent with, too. I still have that $387.90 in my pocket. Even after I add my piddly paycheck to that cash, it isn't enough to cover my rent, so I know the postfee paycheck will leave me even further behind. But it will at least give me *something* to hand to my landlord. Gotta at least let him know I'm trying.

Hopefully, my landlord will still be around by the time I get out of here. It's Friday and this check-cashing line is twelve deep. Only one teller window is open, and as if that isn't bad enough, every transaction is taking twice as long as it should, because everyone has to repeat himself numerous times to be heard correctly through the bulletproof glass.

> Teller: Huh? You have two funny daughters? That's nice.
> Customer: No! Money orders! I need two money orders!

Oh, how do I know the glass is bulletproof? They have a nice big handwritten sign at the top of the glass:

"This Facillity Protected by Buletproof Glass."

Damn! Why don't the owners buy a spelling guide with their profits? Matter of fact, why don't they just remove that sign? That way if someone is stupid enough to try to shoot through it, the bullet will just ricochet and hit the perp right back. We'll rid our society of one more criminal and, as a bonus, there will be one less person in this long-ass line.

Sheesh.

Anyway, I'm the only one standing in here writing, everyone else just kinda looks pissed off. I'm going to keep writing and looking busy, that way no one will talk to me. This place is too small for anyone to be yappin' in my face, 'cause if they have bad breath, I'll be drowning in it until they decide to shut up.

Nope, there is no room for backing up from bad breath in this check-cashing shack. It's about the size of, um, I'd say, a lunch box. I feel like I am the middle bun in the stale double-decker that's inside the lunch box. Poor lunch meat on all sides, just pressing all up against me. I'm developing poor claustrophobia. It's not the poor people, it's the poor atmosphere. I don't want it clinging to my shirt, following me home, and plopping down on my sofa with a drink. It's hitting me how poor this really is: I'm standing in a long line to pay someone to give me my pay. So, technically, they get paid before I do, and it's my damn check.

This is so horrible.

I think I'm going to pass out.

SMACK!

Damn! Who just smacked me in the chin? Everything just went black for a second.

Oh, it wasn't a smack. It was an elbow. This big tree trunk of a guy just elbowed me in the chin while hugging the guy in front of me! Tree Trunk Dude, who has just gotten done cashing his check, turns around, sees guy standing in front of me, yells out, "Heyyyy! George! Good to see you, my man!" while bringing his arms up to execute the macho-man hug/chin slap. Damn, Tree Trunk, this is a small-ass Check-Cashing Joint, not an AA meeting hall. Take the hugs and greetings outside.

I mean, I think it was an accident, but damn, he had to have felt my flesh on his elbow. Can I get an apology?

He's not even looking at me. He's just so glad to see George.

Okay, it doesn't look like I'm going to get that apology. So I'm just going to sit on the bench, out of the hugging tag team's way, and continue writing.

Hello, bench. Hello, nice old lady sitting next to me on this bench. Are you going to start throwing elbow blows, too? Is this some check-cashing initiation I don't know anything about?

I semi-smile at the old lady as I slide onto the bench. No full smiles; this is the 'hood.

What a nice old lady. She starts smiling back. Man, I know she probably has some kids. They should be in here with her. Poor lady clutching her purse like she's cashing Social Security checks for her whole block. Kids should run errands for old folks. Why are you all alone, kind old lady?

Oh, I see why . . . 'cause she's effing insane. A full minute has passed and she's *still* staring at me and *still* smiling. Her eyes are getting wider and wider. Why won't she look away?

Wow, Bench Lady, what's this strange staccato grunt noise you're making? This is so bugged! Her face is totally frozen into a smile, but boy, her voice box is working some overtime.

Grunt. Grunt. Grunt. Grunt.

Grunt.

Grunt. Grunt.

After the grunt series, she immediately transforms the frozen smile into a look of horror and turns away from me. As if I just made those weird noises come out of her mouth. Effing crazy-ass lady!

Twelve people in the check-cashing place and only one person on a bench that holds two people. Maybe three really thin people. I should have known there was a reason no one was sitting on this bench with her.

Oh boy, here she goes again with the sound. Is this her bench or something? Is this the "you're invading my bench" call? You know how sometimes older people have these rituals and all, right? Is that what this is?

God, this throat noise is so weird. It's like a forced, hoarse hiccup.

She keeps on making the noise like she's on a timer. Is anyone else looking at this lady? I look up. Nope, just me.

Oh, now she's stopped.

And now she's starting again. Oh no, this is a different noise.

Sounds kinda like a whistle, except it's coming from her throat. This is, like, a light wheeze.

So now we've gone from the cough to the asthma performance. I should just get up from the bench, but will that make her do some crazier throat trick? Should I clap? Is there a cup to put change in?

I just won't look at her anymore. I'll look at George, the recipient of the hug that made me black out.

Awww, DAMN. George is looking right back at me. And now George is looking at the sliver of space left next to me on the bench like he wants to squeeze on up in there.

Look away, George . . . look away.

Please, George, no. You're too big to sit here.

I knew it. George is coming here to sit in this sliver.

Old Lady is on cough/wheeze intervals now.

Cough. Wheeze. Cough. Wheeze.

George just squeezed into the sliver next to me. Not enough room to maneuver my arm to write now.

Cough. Wheeze.

I'll be back. George keeps glancing at what I'm writing. I know he probably can't read this scribble, but he is really trying. Hi, George.

Gotdamn, George and Wheezy are really trying to ruin what could be a good bench rest (in light of where I am).

I'll finish this when I get home.

When I leave this check-cashing place, I am going to kill my husband. I have the gun under the nightstand.

You'll understand in a minute.

*My husband is one dead man,*

*Angela*

## NOVEMBER 26

Dear Broke Diary:

I'm home now. And don't worry. I'm not killing any husbands. I don't even have one to kill.

I just wrote that because check-cashing George was staring over my shoulder while I was writing. Not peering or trying to sneak a quick peek; he was *reading* what I was writing, line by line.

Guess maybe I did look a little out of place being the only person up in there writing. Well, people were writing down their lottery numbers, but I was scrawling out sentences. Maybe I looked like a cop or something. Or perhaps he thought I was writing about him.

No, George, I was trying to appear unfriendly and closed to conversation. If you're busy, usually no one talks to you. *Usually.*

But George had to squeeze in next to me and practice his literacy skills, so I thought writing of murderous intent would make him keep his mouth shut.

I don't know what made me assume that. It's normal to have a bank account and none of us do, so what's abnormal outside these doors must be normal here. We're society's outcasts. We check cashers have to keep cash under the damn bed like the country is still fighting its way out of the Great Depression.

Guess what George says to me after I wrote that line about killing my husband?

"So you're married, huh?"

"Yes, I'm married," I replied coldly.

"Well, your husband is a lucky man."

No, he's not! I'm going to kill him tonight! Didn't you read what I wrote when you were all up in my notebook?

I wanted to say that out loud, but I'm not crazy. Just can't be up in the Check-Cashing Joint getting smart with people. George's friend had already chin-checked me once, I wasn't about to get another one.

I shoot George a quick, terse smile as my thanks for the compliment.

Wheezy, who has been quiet for the last two minutes, lets out one more noisy breath and gets up to go to the open teller. Good, that means George is next, 'cause this is one conversation that does not need to happen.

"You and your husband live around here?"

Well, obviously George thinks the conversation *does* need to continue. Great.

"Yeah."

Okay now. One-word answers should give him a hint I don't want to converse any longer. Like, how did my plan for an uninterrupted check-cashing experience go awry? I wrote that I was going to kill my damn husband. I know men are hard to figure out, but you'd think that even if they hit on women they know are married, *women who kill* would at least be on their list of women to avoid.

Then again, this brother has no checking account. Maybe the fact that I am obviously literate (I'm writing) and I'm about to be single after my husband passes is a come-up for him. Hard meeting and keeping a woman on a limited budget, I suppose.

Look! Wheezy just finished her transaction. Go, George, go!

George says, "All right, my turn. You take care now." He then pries himself from the bench and approaches the bulletproof glass.

Damn. I'm mean. Maybe he was just being nice.

Aw, who cares? I'm not here to make friends. I don't need any more broke friends. I'm in here to cash this $77.12 paycheck.

Well, I'm here to collect what will be left of that $77.12 after they take out all the damn fees. In addition to the usual fees, this joint got some new and improved fees listed on their handwritten fee sign. With all these fees, you'd think they'd at least be able to afford one professional sign in this place. Some calligraphy. Something. There's a "standard $2.00 check-cashing fee" on top of the "different percentage charge depending on the type of check you are cashing" fee. And what's an "I.D. fee"?

Oh well. I'm next. George is done. That was quick. He must be a regular. He does a quick "bye" salute to me and strolls out the door.

I approach the glass (hey, if it's bulletproof, is it really glass? Isn't one of the properties of glass that it shatters?) and slide my check through the little slot.

"I.D.," the teller says dryly.

No smiles. No "Hello, how are you?" I don't know why she looks so mean. She's not from the 'hood. With all this money she's taking in, I know she scoots right out to the suburbs when the place closes up for the day.

I pull out my driver's license and slip it to her.

She looks at it like it's written in Sanskrit. She alternates between looking at me and looking at my license to gauge whether the girl in the photo who looks just like me really is me.

"Do you have a file here?"

A file? Never even been in this spot before, lady.

"You never cashed a check here? Well, I'll need another form of I.D. Got anything else?"

I pull out my student I.D. and push that to her as well.

That should have brought a smile to her face, but instead she scrunches up her nose like I just slid her a platinum Diarrhea Anonymous membership I.D. or something. Damn, it's just a student I.D., what's with the exaggerated look of disgust??

"What is this?!!" she shouts.

I don't want to reply. I want to fit in here. If I'm a student, everyone in this place will know I'm not really one of them. That breeds contempt. Plus, some people think students have money, and try to rob them. If I were forty and worked forty hours a week only to have to pay all of these fees, I might be tempted to rob a student, too. Shit, they're students, they'll make it back when they graduate.

Dammit. I have to reply. She's waiting on me and she is my last chance to get money from this check.

"It's a student I.D."

"Student I.D.?? That isn't one of our accepted forms of I.D. We'll have to make you an I.D. to put you on file here. That's seven dollars."

Well, guess I just found out what the I.D. fee is, huh?

"Step behind the line and look up at me."

Behind the line? I gotta go to the back of the line to get I.D.?

"The line on the floor . . ."

I look down at the floor. There is a piece of masking tape with "LINE" written on it. I stand behind it and look up at her.

She takes my photo. I'll soon be on file and have a check-cashing I.D. of my very own. The platinum card of the inner city. Woohoo!

After my photo shoot, she picks up my check and starts hitting keys on the calculator.

After that, she reaches into the money drawer and slides me $59.26, along with the receipt from the calculator detailing exactly how a $77.12 check became $59.26.

```
*77.12
 − 3.86 (5%)
 − 7.00 (I.D. fee)
 − 5.00 (first-time check-cashing fee)
 − 2.00 (flat fee)
 _____

 = 59.26
```

"Next!"

I move to the side, put the cash in my pocket, and hustle out of the door to pay this partial rent payment. I know it's against my landlord's policy to pay in cash, but he will have to make an exception this time; I'm not about to drop another dollar on a money order.

I'm fifty dollars short on my rent, but luckily only the landlord's wife is there and I hand her the cash in an envelope and leave before she counts it. I now have $9.26 to last me a week. I could have included that $9.26 in the rent payment, but I had to keep a little bit to last me through the week. Nine dollars and change isn't all that bad to last a regular week, but my gas, electric, and phone bills are overdue this month. Not to mention, I'd like to eat.

No matter what, though, I'm going to keep my head up. I will not become a nude dancer like some of my fellow female students.

*Clothed,*

*Angela*

---

## NOVEMBER 27

Dear Broke Diary:

Well, here I am. Sashaying topless across this table. Hold on, some guy's waving a dollar at me. I'll be back!

Just kidding!!!

No, really, I'm joking!! He's holding up a five-dollar bill!! Woohoo!

Okay, okay, I am entirely, 100 percent joking. I am not in a nudie bar. I am not topless.

I am, however, pretty bottomless. . . .

Um, am I the only person who is walking around without underwear on today?

I know I can't be. This isn't the first time this has happened to me, and I know if it's happened to me more than once, it's happened to someone else at least one time.

I'm three quarters short of clean draws. I still have my $9.26 from yesterday. One quarter. One penny. Nine one-dollar bills.

But, of course, even though the washing machine costs a dollar, it doesn't accept dollar bills, only quarters.

The guy who invented the pay washing machine likes to look down from heaven and see people scamper around in dirty clothes trying to exchange dimes and nickels for quarters. He's probably still bitter that his pay-toilet idea didn't work out. You can hold the door on the way out and let your fellow toileteer in for free, but once the washing machine is done, no more clean clothes until you insert more money.

You can wear jeans a couple times. You can even be a wee bit more skank and don a dirty shirt. Unwashed underwear, however, is a no-go.

When I was growing up, my mom always said, "Whatever you do, always have on clean underwear in case you have to go to the hospital." That's one of those motherly pieces of advice you carry with you forever.

I mean, my mom works in a hospital, she should know. I wonder if she makes fun of people who come in without clean underwear on. Wait, eff clean underwear, what do they do if the patient is like me and has on *no* underwear? Is that a step up or a step down? I'll have to ask her.

Should I pin a note inside my jeans saying, "I normally do wear underwear. Please forgive me, I kinda ran out."

Nope. Can't do that. The paper would be scratching my skin all day, because, well, I have no underwear on.

Someone else has done this, I know. C'mon, admit it. Even so, I'm really paranoid. I feel like people are going to look at the backside of my jeans and tell I'm bare under there.

Janelle was upset one day because she didn't have a matching bra-and-panty set to wear. I don't think I've ever worn a matching set. I'm always mismatched. The sets cost too much money.

So, it's bad enough I have the "unmatching" complex, but today I am really committing a draws faux pas, huh?

I'll just be really careful where I step today. I won't end up in the hospital.

I'll be fine.

With my bare behind.

*Cool breeze,*

*Angie*

---

## NOVEMBER 28

Dear Broke Diary:

Hahahaha! I will never write "I'll be fine" at the end of an entry again!

I wasn't wearing any underwear. I mean, that was supposed to be the defining broke moment of the day. That's it. Nothing else needed to happen.

Yeah, right!

Peep this. . . .

After class, I go to the food court to meet up with Janelle. I see her before she eyes me, but when she does, she rushes out of her chair and runs up to me, dangling a ring of keys in front of my face. Turns out she has her boyfriend's car for the day. Thing is, he doesn't know Janelle only has a learner's permit, and she's kind of scared to drive alone, so she asks me to come with her.

Where is she going?

"To this huge outlet store out in Springfield! I swear, you go in there with ten dollars, you can come out with an entire outfit, shoes and all!"

Her bargain-hunting enthusiasm starts infecting me! Soon I'm hollering, "Yeah, girl! Let's go! I have nine dollars, you think I can get nine tenths of an outfit?!!" like I didn't have another class in two hours.

Well, she was not joking about this store! First of all, it is huge. Like, football-stadium huge. And there are racks and racks of clothes with pink "70% off" tags on them. All of the clothes are designer, but they have the tags cut out of them so you can't tell exactly which designer made 'em. I guess the designer did that because these were irregulars and they didn't want whatever store bought them to try to resell them for normal price.

My $9 *could* get me a whole outfit, but all of the shirts under $3 have major stain or rip damage. I do find a perfect pair of pants for $7 and start to rush to the fitting room, but Janelle asks me to wait for her so I can give her feedback on her outfits.

I look through other racks while I'm waiting for her. She has $30, so she could be a while. I don't see any other pants as nice as the ones in my arms. Lined wool pants for $7? Almost unbelievable. And with a cute little cuff. Cuffs look so cute with boots. Aw, man, if these fit, they will be my new favorite pants! I'm going to be the shit!

Janelle finally comes over to me hugging a bundle of clothes to her body. We're ready to try on our bargain fashion finds.

After the fitting-room attendant counts our items, Janelle and I stroll into the try-on area.

Shit.

There was no indication that these were communal dressing rooms.

I bust out laughing. There is just nothing else to do.

I have no underwear on. I have one pair of perfect pants to try on.

How am I going to try on these pants?

If it was just me and Janelle, I might have explained the situation and just tried to hurry up and throw the pants on before anyone else came in the dressing room. But it's not just me and Janelle. It's me, Janelle, and about six other women in various stages of undress.

Know what? Nope, I wouldn't even have told Janelle. She tripped out on me when she found out I don't wear matching bra-and-panty sets, so I really don't want to deal with her reaction when she finds out I am totally without briefs. (Next time I run out of draws, I'll go braless, too. That'll count as having on a matching set, right?)

Man, I really wish these were stalled dressing rooms. Yeah, I would have tried them on without underwear. I didn't mean for this to happen and I'm clean, thank you. How do you know the woman who tried them on before me didn't have sores on her legs? Or that woman in the corner pulling the sweater over her head, she could have a gang of head lice in her wig. You never know.

Damn, I will never find a pair of pants like this again. And I have no working car and no way to get back out here to return them if they don't fit.

Okay, it's obvious I can't try them on, so the dilemma now becomes: How am I going to leave the fitting room without trying them on and not look crazy?

I must have been standing there with the pants in my hands longer than I thought.

Janelle has on an entire outfit already, looks up at me, and pipes up, "Why haven't you tried your pants on? Try 'em on! They'll look great! You have to try 'em on, you can't return stuff here."

"No, I really don't like them anymore."

"Aw, don't be self-conscious. No one will be looking at you!"

Oh, trust me. When I take my pants down and expose naked ass, everyone will be looking at me!

"No, Janelle, you know, I don't like them anymore, and I don't really need more winter pants. Spring will be here soon."

"Ang, you're bugging out. Spring is months away. The pants are seven dollars. Try them on."

If she doesn't shut up . . . I hate lying. I should just drop my pants and be like, "Here, dammit. This is why I can't try them on! *Naked ass.* I needed quarters. Next time I ask you for quarters, give 'em up, okay?!"

Of course I don't do that. Public place, naked ass, and yelling at someone really isn't cool.

"No, Janelle, I only have nine dollars to last me the week. I need paper towels and bath tissue more than I need pants."

She starts to protest, but I hurriedly tell her I'll catch her out front. I know she'll be mad because she wants me to help her decide which outfit to get, but I have to step out of there before she offers to buy the pants for me (she's been holding on to this $30 for three days and is feeling really rich). If she offered that, I'd be stuck thinking up an excuse about why I couldn't try on free pants.

She actually isn't mad that I didn't stay to give her feedback on her outfits. She says I am acting "a bit weird," and I am. I can't stop laughing because the situation is so surreal, but I can't tell her why I'm laughing.

Ah, my life.

*Need Underoos,*

*Angie*

---

## NOVEMBER 29

Dear Broke Diary:

Old landlords rule!

Oh, not old meaning "former" or "previous"; old like senior-citizen old. Old like AARP gold-card old. Old like "I'd tell you a story about what it was like when I went to school . . . but I don't remember. Have you seen my pills?" old.

That's Mr. Aiello. My current landlord. Too bad this is a sublet or I'd stay here forever. (Or until he kicked me out like my last landlord.)

You know how that whole bounced debit card / ChexSystems / check-cashing fee-asco left me with not enough money to pay my rent in full, so I left what cash I had with Mr. Aiello's wife, right? I gave her some cash in an envelope. Oh, I told you this already. Sorry.

Anyway, Mr. Aiello, God bless his soul, stopped by today. He only drops by to collect money, so I was sure this wasn't just a friendly visit. He came to get his dough.

He knocks on the door and comes in all red-faced and sweaty. He's also somewhat out of breath. I bet walking up all those steps got to him. Before he opens his mouth, I tell him he looks exhausted and offer him some water.

He starts to refuse. "Oh no. I just came by to get—"

"No, I insist. Sit. Your face is red. Let me get you some water."

He reluctantly sits down. I pour a glass of water and hand it to him.

The phone rings. I turn my back to him to grab the receiver from the wall. When I swing back around, his head is drooping forward and his eyes are closed.

Mr. Aiello is nodding off!

I tell the bill collector that I can't talk at the moment. I pivot and hang the phone back in the receiver.

When I face Mr. Aiello this time, his head is tilted back and his mouth is wide open.

Mr. Aiello is asleep. On my couch. Somehow, he is still holding the glass of water upright.

I lean in closer to check for normal breathing sounds. He's breathing.

Is the ol' potbelly still rising and falling? It is.

So I leave.

And lock the door. (He has a key.)

I'm back now. He's gone.

I am sure he is too embarrassed to come over again.

And if his wife calls me because she notices he came back empty-handed? I still have the upper hand: Her husband slept at my house.

"Oh yes, Mrs. Aiello. I sure did settle that account. He fell asleep right afterwards. *Men.* Only a man would come over to collect a debt and then turn the visit into a private slumber party. Young and old, they're all the same, eh? Take care, Mrs. Aiello."

Sure, she'd be slack-jawed for a moment. Might even confront her man about his new collection practices. They'd work it all out, though.

Lovers' spats end. Eviction, however, is forever.

Thanks again, Mr. Aiello.

*Angie*

---

DECEMBER 1

Dear Broke Diary:

It's time for a rant.

You know what? I swear if I didn't have to work so much, I'd start that damn Broke Student Union. I've already changed the charter twice in my head.

Our main goal would be to get rid of stupid students. Quantum physics geniuses who lack common sense are downright dangerous. Not to mention, they cost us *all* money.

While I was walking to work today, I passed a mob of students protesting outside of the university president's office. They were screaming that the university doesn't keep them safe. That too many students are getting robbed by petty criminals in the surrounding neighborhood. That they should be able to walk drunk and shirtless at 3:00 A.M. through city streets with an open wallet dangling from their left nipple.

"Protect us, University! The walking escort service, the driving escort service, the fifty new security guards and thirty new cops just aren't enough! Someone still got robbed! Protect us!"

These chanting students are costing me money. They are going to convince the university to begin another multimillion-dollar safety initiative. Which the university will, of course, pass on to us. I mean me. I'm paying tuition with interest here, you little protesters! Your friend got robbed of fifty dollars? Well, for each new initiative you convince the university to implement, I'm probably out about a thousand dollars.

I'm tired of these college kids taking my income. Robbing me. The Broke Student Union's goal would be to convince the administration to discipline these protesting students before they cause any more financial harm.

If broke students can be forced to take time off via "Financial Hold" 'cause they can't pay tuition, then these chanting picket-sign students who keep tuition rising should be held accountable, too.

Matter of fact, the students who get robbed after dark, off campus, during hours of the university escort operation should be punished as well. If I can get a D for messing up a ten-page paper, someone who *walks* through the inner city wearing a "Wharton" shirt, when he had the option of having a university van pick him up and take him wherever he needed to go, deserves some time off. We'll put him on Common Sense Hold.

If the university gives in to the protesters' demands but ignores the cry of the tiny Broke Student Union, we'll have to find another way to recoup the money we've lost to the new safety initiative. We could take pictures of the protesting students and develop them into a manual called "Easy Targets." We'd distribute it for free at area high schools.

Yeah, I just saw on the news that a lot of public schools don't have books (could be why some of their students end up robbing folks), so not only would our "Easy Targets" initiative be providing broke students with the personal satisfaction of having helped the community, it'd be helping neighborhood eleventh-graders learn how to read!

Now, before people start screaming at me, the "Easy Targets" manual wouldn't encourage violent crimes. I grew up in Philly. Most people I know, including myself, have been robbed before. It's not fun. Thing is, when we got robbed, we didn't have door-to-door university-escort vans at our disposal. These students do, yet they still protest. They *are* Easy Targets, and whatever is made off of them, whether it be by three-card monte, or going door-to-door selling stale Snickers, the money will be split with the Broke Student Union to help us pay for whatever tuition increase they cause.

Jeez, I bet the university will even pay a marketing team to come up with some new slogan for their multimillion-dollar safety initiative.

I've got a slogan for them: "Be safe! If the people who live in the damn neighborhood are afraid to walk the streets at night, maybe you should be, too!"

It's that simple.

Now give me my check.

Thanks for listening.

*Ang*

---

DECEMBER 17

Dear Broke Diary:

Oh boy! Nothing like holiday time at the office. Maybe I shouldn't say "the office," because that sounds so official, like I have a real job or something. Nope, "the office" is the place I work at fifteen hours a week for about two burgers above fast-food wages. I don't really work for "the office"; I work for the government under what's known as the Federal Work-Study Program. You know, the "these could have been fifteen extra *studying* hours, but you're poor so you have to *work*" program?

But, once again, I digress.

Today is "Sign up to bring something to the holiday party" day. Because I don't come in until midafternoon, most of the slots on the sign-up board are already taken. John, the head manager, has signed up to bring a bottle of Diet Coke. That cheap bastard. That's what I wanted to sign up for.

Sandy, the secretary, bounces over to me. She's just too damn happy. It's the fake "holiday happy" thing people do. Argh.

"Annnnngieeeee!! Hi!"

She adjusts her elf hat.

"We need you to sign up to bring something for the party. Looks like everything is taken except for the dessert. Could you do that?"

"No, Sandy. I haven't been able to afford dessert for over a year, so if I do make some, I won't be sharing it. Thanks for asking, though!"

Then I start whistling "Rudolph the Red-Nosed Reindeer" and walk back to my desk.

Oh, come on. You know I didn't say that. I wanted to, though. Hell, I should be *allowed* to say that. I'm a pseudo-employee; I don't have to be a team player. I should just be able to sit on the bench and wear the uniform. I shouldn't have to bring dessert.

If this is their way of making me feel a part of the office, why

don't they skip inviting me to the party and just give me a holiday bonus like everyone else?

But, damn, I gotta work here, and if I say no, it'll be all over
the office.

Okay, here goes.

"Yes, of course I can bring the dessert."

Ooh! Look! I just made Sandy's day!

"Well, that's just great, Angieeee! Like, what do you think
you could make??"

My brain is yelling, Say "Jell-O" before it's too late! Say "Jell-
O"! Jell-O or Slim Jims! Jell-O or Slim Jims! C'mon now!

"How about a chocolate cheesecake?" I reply.

As soon as I hear those words fall from my lips, I want to suck
them back up.

What the . . . ??? Chocolate cheesecake? Cast these demons
out of me!! Where did that come from?

I know exactly where it came from. The Ghost of Boring Office Jobs Present. I've been playing "Fantasy Food" and searching for gourmet recipes on the Internet instead of the usual
mind-stimulating data-entry crap. Yesterday I found a chocolate cheesecake recipe and promised myself I was going to try
it as soon as I got some money.

I was going to try it.

*For myself.*

*Just for me.*

Not for cheap-ass Diet Coke John and the rest of this effin'
office.

Oh well, the words were out of my mouth; the damage was
done. Sandy had jingled her bells on over to write "Angie:
chocolate cheesecake" on the dry-erase board.

There goes a week's pay.

Now, let me get back online and look these ingredients up.

*Surfin'*,

*Angie*

---

DECEMBER 18

CHOCOLATE CHEESECAKE
8 ounces Oreo cookie crumbs
2 ounces butter, melted
3 pounds cream cheese
12 ounces granulated sugar
9 eggs
1 tablespoon vanilla, to taste
1 cup heavy cream
8 ounces dark chocolate, chopped

Dear Chef Broke Diaree:

I couldn't find the recipe online, so I got my cooking home-girl to hook me up with a recipe she uses.

Pre–cheesecake ingredients shopping, I had $28 to last me the week. I now have 59 cents. The total for the cheesecake ingredients came to $27.41. I barely made it.

I can't believe I had to buy a whole bottle of vanilla. A bottle of vanilla is for someone who uses vanilla, like regularly. I think I'll just take the spoonful out I need for the recipe and return the rest of the bottle to the store. Would they even notice? I'll tell them it tasted chocolatey or something. I need that $1.79.

ARGH! I can't believe I even think about things like that. This is terrible. Will there ever be a day when $1.79 doesn't seem like so much money?

Anyway, I'm supposed to be telling you about how I made this effin' stupid cheesecake.

Everything started off fine, especially since Carmen lent me her springform pan. (Yeah, like I'm going to buy a pan that limits itself to the preparation of one food! Frying pan: cool. Pot: cool. Springform pan: yeah, right.) I dunno about you, but I get this power rush when I'm cooking something that requires mixing and measuring. I had all the recipe ingredients laid on the counter, and I had to step back like "Yeah! I'm about to mold these and make a whole new food!" Like, "I'm making a new food out of food. How cool is that? I'm a cook!"

The crust was easy. I just mixed the crumbs and the melted butter, slapped the melted mixture into the springform pan, and heated it for five minutes.

The cake part was a bit more challenging. Nowhere on this damned recipe did it say I needed a blender or a mixer. Nowhere! It just said:

"Mix the 3 pounds of cream cheese with the sugar until smooth."

I was a mixing, hurtin'-arm fool. I had to take mix breaks, my arms were so sore.

Cream cheese is not creamy. Cream cheese is damn hard. Plus, the cheap spoon I stole from the cafeteria kept bending under the mixing pressure. I know I'm not paying all this tuition for second-rate silverware.

All in all, the mixing took damn near an hour. I'm surprised the cream cheese didn't get moldy sitting out so long. I bet people notice my arms are a bit more buff, though. I'm going to wear a muscle shirt tomorrow. So what if it's snowing?

After that upper-body mixing workout, I obey the directions and pour my creamy mixture into two separate bowls. Easy.

Now I gotta make something called "ganache." This is the first time in my life I have ever seen this word. It looks snooty. Like some new European clothing designer.

"Be sexy . . . in Ganache Jeans!"

I should have known by the stuck-up name that the ganache was going to be a problem. I hate snooty food.

"To prepare the ganache, bring the heavy cream to a boil, then add the chocolate. Pour half of the ganache into one of the bowls of cheesecake mixture and mix."

I can do that. Simple. What's next?

"Place the other half of the ganache in a small bowl to the side."

See, man!!! Eff a ganache! I knew she was going to cause problems. A small bowl to the side? How many bowls does this recipe think I have?

This is a two-bowl household here, Ganache. I live in one room. There will never be more than two people over here at once, therefore I only need two bowls. And one is full of all that cream cheese I just stirred. How are you going to come into my house and try to take over both bowls? Ganache: *I made you.* Not the other way around. Have you forgotten that?

Hold up. I'm trippin'. Cursing out a bowl-less ganache. Is it my fault or Ganache's? Should I have read the actual *process* of making the cheesecake before I decided to make it? I only read the ingredients.

Well, none of that matters now. I need a place to pour this ganache.

I start looking frantically throughout the kitchen, like I think there really might be a hidden supply of bowls I forgot I purchased. I know there isn't!!! I'd never waste money on something as stupid as a third bowl!! Then why can't I stop looking? What the hell am I going to do? I really only have two bowls, and both of my stovetop pots (which, of course, can sub for bowls) now have stuff in them. Dammit, man!!!

Okay. I have no more bowls. Point-blank. Next question: What do I have that looks like a bowl? What do I have that can hold liquid like a bowl does?

Nothing.

I even contemplate pouring it on a paper plate. Naw, I can't do that.

Ganache has won.

I look down at the floor.

No, I can't do that. I *can't* . . .

I have no choice.

I empty my cat's water bowl and clean it out.

Awww! Stop your whining and cringing. Let's be rational about this. Cats are clean. And the cat never actually touches the bowl. The *water* touches the bowl, the cat laps at the water. When you eat in a restaurant, how can you be sure the person who drank out of your cup last didn't have a cold sore or anything? How do you know how well they clean their cups and bowls? I cleaned the bowl thoroughly, and in the process cleaned my conscience of all guilt.

Thanks to the cat's water bowl, the ganache was great, the

cake was great, what people don't know won't hurt 'em, and everyone was happy, okay?

Oh, hell no, I didn't actually *eat* any of the cake. Of course, Sandy came over to me twice chirping, "Your cake is so good! You should have some!" Haha.

"No, no . . . I want to make sure everyone gets to have at least two slices!! Yeah, I'm sure! No, no, really. I'm fine! I made another one, and it's home in the fridge waiting for me! But thanks!"

Plus, you know, I was so full off of John's scrumptious Diet Coke, I really couldn't fit in any of the cake. I did lick the batter from the bowl last night, so it's not like I was trying to poison anyone!

And it's not like they'll ever find out. And it was the water bowl, not the food bowl. And dammit, I just did what I had to do to contribute to the office party. Gotta be a team player, you know? And hell, I'm tiring of rationalizing this. They should have known better than to let the student worker make the dessert.

So whatever.

Pass the Diet Coke.

*Burp,*

*Angie*

---

JANUARY 2

Dear Broke Diary:

There is nothing worse than being broke on New Year's Eve.

Being penniless on Christmas is cool. I actually made peace

with that holiday a long time ago. Everyone always says, "Oh, you don't have to get me anything." And I don't.

But New Year's Eve causes me to stress a little bit. I have never had a fun New Year's Eve. Fun ones cost money.

(Wait, before I start, let me warn you this entry will be long. It's winter break, my friends are all in different cities, and it's freezing outside. I have no homework to do and, of course, no money. I'm just plain bored. So grab some cocoa or something and read on. Thanks.)

Last New Year's Eve, my now ex-boyfriend and I involuntarily baby-sat his nieces and nephews. The kids' parents swore they were just going to the store. They didn't get back until the next day. Guess it's hard finding an open store on New Year's Eve, huh?

It's not like me and the ex had any real plans. We were both broke, so we were just going to have an intimate evening. Thanks to his family, all we got intimate with were *Sesame Street* books and sock puppets.

Year before that I was laid up on a hospital emergency-room stretcher, blind in one eye and orange cat hair all over my face. Drunk people all around me. Everyone else covered in multi-colored confetti. I was covered in orange cat hair.

I'd just adopted my cat and snuck him into the dorm room. I was waiting for my boyfriend to get off work so we could go out. I was watching the clock and having fun playing with my new orange ball of furry love. I sat on the couch, held a shoestring in front of the cat, and watched as his eyes darted from side to side while he prepared to attack the string.

I was leaning over into his face talking to him. He was just so adorable!

"Good kitty kitty. Yeah! Grab that string! Such a cute kitty. OW SHIT, KITTY!!! GET YOUR CLAW OUT OF MY EYEBALL!!!!"

Everything went orange. I felt like my brain was being pulled in two different directions.

I believe the cat either tired of the game or decided my "cute kitty" voice was annoying. Whatever it was, cute kitty's claw had missed the string and hooked right into my eye.

Do you know what it feels like when a cat claws into your eye like he's attacking string?

Debilitating, savage pain. It felt like every nerve ending in my body had relocated to my eye. I had no other body part except my left eye. I was one big eyeball rolling around the room in pain. Each time I tried to blink, it felt like a razor blade was attached to the inside of my eyelid, and my eye was spewing out more water than an open fire hydrant.

I had to crawl to the phone to call campus police to drive me to the E.R.

I spent seven hours in the E.R. I had a corneal abrasion and was forced to wear these paper wraparound sunglasses for a week. I looked like a nutcase with those big-ass paper shades on. I had daily visits to the ophthalmologist for two weeks afterwards. He always had an officeful of students he'd gather around to stare into my eye. They'd inevitably say things like "Wow" and "Look, you can see where the claw went in and where it came out again!" They'd usually gasp for several minutes, too. Afterwards, the doc would try to lift my spirits and offer support.

"Don't worry, it'll heal. The eye is a very resilient muscle."

Thanks, Doc. Happy New Year!

Well, after all my other festive Father Time celebrations, I don't know what made me think this one would be any better.

My car was working again (my brother's present to me! Thanks, bro!), so I drove two hours to be with my boyfriend in Maryland, and we broke up about four hours before the New Year.

Great, what do I do now?

I guess I'll be doing nothing.

The same nightclubs that let ladies in free before 10:00 P.M. 364 nights out of the year suddenly charge hundreds of dollars just to get in the door tonight.

Same deejay, same people, same music, all at a higher price because it is New Year's Eve. So, no club for me. I have $10 to my name, and that's for the gas and tolls back to Philly.

I dunno. Maybe something will come up. I call my friend Abby, who moved to D.C. after graduating. She's probably still broke, having been a liberal-arts major and all. My suspicions are right, she's still broke (surviving off temp-agency gigs) and has no plans. Last time I hung out with Abby in D.C., we were trying to get into this club called Republic Gardens before 10:00 P.M. (ladies free!), but we got there at 10:05 and we had to go all the way back home. We didn't have the $5 cover charge. The door guy asked us for the $5 and we just turned and walked away. I tried to mumble something about having to go to an ATM so we didn't look *so* bad, but it didn't matter. We were humiliated.

Well, we'll try to make up for that tonight. I know a couple of other people in the area. I decide to call Randy. Randy is one of those cool male buddies every woman should have. Male buddies give away male secrets, help you move things; you know, they're like brothers. Well, except you can tell them stuff you can't tell Brother, 'cause Brother will tell your parents. Randy is usually broke, but he knows a lot of artsy musical people. Maybe he knows of some free pseudo-hippie gatherings or something.

When I get him on the phone, I tell him about my little breakup. After offering consolations, he says he's headed to a bar with two of his friends. Friends I've never met. He says he will lend me enough money so that me and Abby can come along. How nice of him!

I call Abby back and she's down to go even though I give her a long warning about how I only know Randy and have no idea what the other dudes are going to be like.

I've already got on my only dress pants, since I thought I'd be heading out with my now-ex, so I rush right out the door to pick her up, then we head over to Randy's house.

I ring the bell and my buddy Randy answers the door in a tan corduroy sport coat. I've never seen Randy wear a button-up shirt, much less a sport coat. And what's with the tan corduroy? He looks like a pimp in training. As uncomfortable as the sport jacket is to look at, he looks even more uncomfortable in it.

While my eyes are following the pattern of the corduroy, another guy comes to the door behind Randy. He introduces himself as Charles. He's kinda cute. No corduroy in his New Year's Eve ensemble, but a cutie nonetheless.

We all exchange introductions, then start the all-important conversation about whose car is the most likely to last through an entire night. Turns out Third Guy, who hasn't arrived yet, has a real job and a real car with power windows and all. We designate his car as limo of the night before he even shows up.

We all sit and start chitchatting about nothing while we're

waiting for Third Guy to arrive. I notice Randy seems really un-comfortable. Must be the corduroy collar scratching the back of his neck. All jokes aside, he looks really sad. I wonder what's wrong? I guess I'll ask him later when we're alone.

Finally Third Guy arrives. We tell him he is the designated driver, then we all pile into his ride and start our adventure.

This is cool! I'm actually going out on New Year's Eve. I'm so excited!

Wait, I'm in Third Guy's car and I don't even know his name. Third Guy, what's your name again?

(He said some beautiful West African–sounding name that I'm not even going to embarrass myself by attempting to spell.)

I'm mesmerized by his name. "Oh wow, that sounds exotic! What does it mean?"

"It's the day of the week I was born. In my village you are named for the day of the week you were born."

Fascinating! I have to know more!

"So, what day were you born?"

"Wednesday."

Okay, this is too cool. I love other cultures. He's named after a day of the week! Just one more question:

"So, when someone in the village yells your name, does one seventh of the village turn around?"

Bwahahah!!! I'm a funny gal, I tell you! That should loosen everyone up and get the conversation flowing!

Hey, why am I the only one laughing? Why does Charles sigh and suddenly drop his head into his lap? Why does Randy look even more depressed?

Okay, somebody, please laugh! Someone at least say something to break this weird silence. We keep driving.

Finally we stop at a red light and Wednesday turns all the way around in his seat to look at me. He opens his mouth and begins to answer my question in the most deadpan, flattest voice I have ever heard. "No. They do not. One seventh of the village does not turn around. Respect my people." Then he slowly rolls his eyes at me, turns around, and faces the windshield again.

*Okeydokey.*

Wow, this uncomfortable silence in the air? Yeah, that'd be my fault.

Wait, hold up. I was just making a joke. Eff Wednesday. Don't tell me about a stupid custom and not expect me to make fun of it. Shit, I'm an anthropology major, and even with all my sensitivity training, I know naming kids after days of the week is a crazy wack custom that can only lead to chaos. I should take another jab at his weak week name, just to shatter this silence if nothing else. I'd do it, too! If only Randy didn't look like he was about to throw up.

Abby must feel a joke welling up in me. She shoots me a "Please don't get us kicked out of this car" look.

Okay, fine, I'll keep my mouth shut. Seems like everyone else has their jaw on lockdown, too, 'cause we ride a wave of silence right on into the bar.

Wow! The bar is packed! No, not this bar, some other bar someplace else. There are about twelve people here. I hope Randy isn't wasting that custom corduroy outfit on such a sparse crowd.

Oh well, I'm not complaining. If Randy hadn't been nice enough to lend me this money, I'd be sitting in an apartment wallowing in breakup sorrow. I'm going to order a drink. Um, okay, I have no money, so I'm going to hope someone else orders me a drink.

Charles, the cutie friend, asks what I want to drink. Such a gentleman! I wonder if he's single. The drink is good and the bar is actually starting to fill up. This could be an okay night! I wish we could get rid of Wednesday, but I'll let him stay 'cause he's driving and all.

Hey, a band even starts playing! They're jamming some wacky D.C. go-go music, but it's still a live band.

I swing around from checking out the live band and well, *lookee here!* The bartender is smiling at me. This is very good. Bartenders make drinks. He slides over, extends his hand, and introduces himself. Hi, Paul. I'm Angie. Yes, I'd very much like a glass of that expensive wine for free. These guys, no, they are just friends. I don't even like that one in the gray shirt. He's named after a day of the week and is very bitter about it. Thanks for the wine, Paul.

Abby is looking at my wine like a hungry beggar child would look at a cheese sandwich. Shoot, I got her in here for free, she can at least scheme her way into some free alcohol. Go on, girl! Smile at the old drunk guy at the end of the bar who looks like he's been here since last New Year's Eve. You can do it, girl! Have confidence!

Aww, damn. She's still looking at my wine. I know she's broke. I'll try to get Paul to give her some.

Hold on . . . why is Wednesday giving me the evil eye now? I

thought everything was settled. Let me ask him why he's looking at me like that.

"Hey, what's up? Something wrong with me?"

"Is that your second drink?" he sneers. "You really need to
slow down."

I set my drink down on the bar, 'cause the fury I'm about to
unleash on Mr. Wednesday is going to knock him into Thursday. He'll have to change his name. I can't believe he just said
that to me.

"Slow down? I have two drinks and you're telling me to slow
down? It's fuckin' New Year's Eve! Stop being so uptight! And
you know what? Just don't say shit to me for the rest of the
night. You're not ruining my night." I raise my hand to sum-
mon Paul. "Paul? Can I have another drink, please?"

*Slow down?* How the hell is he gonna tell me to slow down
after two New Year's Eve drinks? If you can't speed up on New
Year's Eve, when can you? During Lent? Dumb-ass.

Oh damn, here's that silence again. Randy, who has had
only one drink so far, looks like he is about to pass out. Yes, I
just cursed out your friend. Sorry, Randy. Charles just stares at
me. I stare back to see if he has any comments that deserve furious replies.

"Damn" is all the commentary Charles offers.

After about three more minutes of unspoken tension,
Charles attempts to break the silence barrier. "Well, since the
night is off to such a frolicking start, let's all dance or something."

I'm not trying to dance. I'm staying here and securing my
seat at Paul's "Free Drinks for Angie" bar. Plus, I need to keep

my eye on Wednesday before he tries to drive off and leave me here. He needs to loosen up. He's probably just mad because no girls are talking to him. Matter of fact, c'mon, Abby, walk me to the ladies' room so I can write "12/31: Warning! Don't talk to the guy at the bar in the gray silk shirt! He's got bad village customs" in lipstick on the mirrors.

When Abby and I emerge from the bathroom, we see Randy and Charles engaged in lively conversation. Or rather, Charles is trying to have a lively conversation with a still-downtrodden-looking Randy, who looks like he's five years old and his best friend just moved seven states away. When Charles sees us approaching, he stops talking and kinda nudges Randy in our direction.

Why does Randy look afraid to speak to me? Man, what's wrong with him? I walk over and ask him why he isn't talking to any of the women in the bar. He sighs. Man, I'm not going to let my buddy Randy ruin this one chance at a fun New Year's night. I just go on and keep talking to Abby. Out of the corner of my eye, I see Charles giving him what appears to be a pep talk and another nudge in my direction.

Finally, Randy shuffles over to me and opens his mouth.

In the weirdest affected pseudo-British accent, he asks, "Ahngela, would you like to dahnce?"

Wow, what, was Charles nudging Randy to try out his "Millionaire Soap Opera Accent in a Box" technique on me? He sounded just like Victor from *The Young and the Restless*. Why is he acting so weird? I would actually dance with him, but the band is still playing that go-go music. People in D.C. have these special dances they do with go-go music, and if you don't know the dance you look as out of place as a couple waltzing across the floor during "The Electric Slide."

I don't know how to dance to go-go music. Randy knows I am go-go challenged, but I'll remind him anyway.

"Randy, come get me when they start playing Prince again! You know I don't want to embarrass you with me not knowing this go-go stuff!"

"Okay," he replies. A faint smiles floats across his face.

Two minutes later, the same song is still on. He asks me again if I'd like to "dahnce." I wish he'd kill that weird voice. Did someone spike his drink?

No, I don't want to dance to the go-go music, so stop-stop asking me, please?

All these women in here, I know he can get one to dance with him. Why waste the night on me?

I feel a tap on my shoulder. Bartender Paul is handing me a slip of paper. Aw, man. This better not be a bill. If it is, Bartender Paul is in for a big surprise.

Whew, it's not. It's Paul's phone number. Cool. The night is not a total waste. Being broke is okay if you have friends in the right places. Like, behind bars. When bartenders like you, you always have a place to go. Where everybody knows your name. And they're always glad you came.

As soon as Charles sees Bartender Paul handing me his number, he shakes his head and throws me a look of disgust.

Charles says, "I *know* you're not trading phone numbers with the bartender."

"Why not?"

He repeats himself, only a little louder this time.

"I *know* you're not trading phone numbers with the bartender." He motions his head towards Randy.

Oh. *Oh no.* Please don't tell me that by Randy loaning me and Abby money to come tonight, this means I am his date. No one told me that. So wait, are both me and Abby his date or is it just me? See, that's why I hate not having my own money. There's always a catch to someone loaning you some. Buddies cease to be buddies once that money transaction goes down. I guess that's what has happened with me and Randy. But to be sure, I'mma ask him.

"Randy, do you like me or something? Is this a date because you loaned me money?"

Charles slaps the palm of his hand against his forehead like I shouldn't have asked Randy that.

"No, this isn't a date. Yes, of course I like you. You're a good friend. A wonderful person."

Charles slaps his forehead once again. I slap my number down on the bar for Paul. Someone behind me slaps a shiny paper "Happy New Year" hat atop my head.

Suddenly, everyone starts counting down backwards. Oh! This must be what crowds do when they celebrate New Year's together. I want to count, too!

"Seven . . . six . . . five . . . four . . . three . . . two . . . one . . . Happy New Year!!!"

Drunken sloppy hugs are exchanged all around the bar. I turn to hug Charles and Randy and then glide over to hug Wednesday, even though he chastised me for drinking two drinks. It's a new year. Let's start fresh.

Wednesday gives me a weak, halfhearted hug, looks down at his watch, and says, "It's 12:01, let's get out of here, y'all."

What??!! Well, he's not playing. Got his coat on, keys out and everything. Let's go. He's the driver. He calls the shots. Oh well. At least I made it to 12:01. No kids, and no orange cat hair.

Charles suggests we all go get our cars from in front of Randy's house, follow him back to his apartment, and have a "New Year's Eve talk."

Okay, that sounds a little nerdy, but I'm down. I don't have a damn thing else to do.

We get to Charles's place and the talking vibe just isn't there. I mean, Wednesday is mad at me and Randy is still sporting that sad, nauseated look. Abby just looks glad to be out of the damn house and Charles keeps moving his eyes between my face and Randy's. Well, what he can see of Randy's face, considering Randy has his head between his knees.

I can't take this uncomfortable silence anymore. This is the one night of the year we can make as much noise as we want, and it's quieter than a little mute girl's backyard tea party with her imaginary friends.

You know what? I'm going to say something. Something profound, something great and meaningful. Let the silence be broken!

"So, did everybody have fun tonight? Let's hear it for New Year's Eve! Yeah!"

My enthusiasm is met with laughter and groans. After the laughter dies, I just hear groans. All coming from Randy. The groans are muffled by his thigh. He still hasn't lifted his head from his lap.

Randy is freaking me out. And I know he's not drunk. He only had one drink. Let me ask him what's wrong.

"Yo, Randy, what's the matter? Are you hot? Let me take off your sport coat."

Randy moans some quick, unintelligible babble into his thigh. Charles starts darting his eyes between us again. Wednesday sees Charles's eyes and chuckles a bit while saying, "Don't do it, man. Don't go off on her."

Charles abruptly stands up. "Yes! I *will* do it to her! I *will* go off on Angie. She deserves it." Charles then turns and tosses me the meanest, coldest look I have ever seen. I've only known him about three hours now.

"Angie, you want to know why Randy is hurting? Why he is speaking in grunts instead of full sentences? YOU!" He slowly outstretches his arm and points a dramatic index finger in my direction. "You have emasculated my friend Randy all night long."

Hold the hell up. Grrr . . . I've *emasculated* Randy? Wow, I didn't even think I brought my scalpel to the bar. I hate arguing with college students who use those big words. Why couldn't he just say "I think you hurt Randy." And I know Charles is still an undergrad; why is he practicing for the bar already? Standing up, pointing at me, accusing me of shit like this is a jury trial or something. Well, pass me my Bible, because I'm about to testify, Your Honor.

"I'm emasculating Randy?? For God's sake! What are you talking about?"

Charles wearily shakes his head. "You know Randy likes you. He paid for you and your girlfriend to get into the bar, and you gave your number to Paul the bartender! You are the reason good guys get hurt all time!" Each time he says "you," he points at me.

Wednesday lets out a cheer. A cheer for the good guys, I suppose. Randy, head still hanging, lets out the biggest sigh yet. That's the first sigh I understand. It is the "get me out of here, I can't believe this is happening" sigh.

Charles keeps up the attack. "I am so tired of my friends being taken advantage of!"

I'm pissed now, because he keeps going on and on about how the bad guys always win, as if I'm the most horrible, conniving woman on the planet because Randy lent me the money to get into the club and I got a phone number. As long as Randy's been my friend, he's never ever told me he liked me romantically. Let me jump up so I can look Charles in the eye. I need a good comeback, because this isn't fair.

"You're mean!" I scream at Charles.

Whoa. Not quite the comeback I wanted. Let me try again, because Charles and Wednesday are actually laughing at that comeback. I hear Abby yell a supportive "Yeah!" but I suppose she is just doing that because she knows I will leave her here with these losers if she doesn't side with me.

Let me come back a little harder.

"Randy lent money to me to pay for me *and* Abby! Does that mean if Abby got a phone number, she is emasculating him, too? Or is it just me? And the bigger issue is RANDY NEVER TOLD ME HE LIKED ME!"

Charles throws his hands up like arguing with me is just a lost cause because I'm stupid. Stupid Angie.

"You should have known he liked you!" Charles yells. Wednesday starts cheering Charles on, as if we're boxing and all his money is on Charles.

"How could I have known if he didn't say shit??" I holler back.

"He wore a sport coat tonight, for Christ's sake!"

"Since when is a sport coat an indicator of romantic intent?! Is corduroy the new 'fabric of romance' or some shit??!!"

And on and on and on and on the fight went. Charles has a real thing against women. I start crying. I'm yelling at Charles, telling him I just broke up with my man and don't need him comparing me to all the evil women he's ever known.

It takes thirty minutes of Charles screaming hard-core accusations at me, thirty grueling minutes in which my voice turns hoarse and Charles's neck veins are about to explode, thirty minutes before Randy lifts his head from his lap and chirps out, "Stop fighting, you guys. It's okay."

It's okay? What's okay? Eff that. I'm still fighting, but now I want to fight Randy for even bringing me out tonight.

"Randy, did I emasculate you??!!"

"No, you didn't."

Charles sighs and starts screaming at Randy. "Yes she did! She castrated you! You lent her money and she gave her number to Paul the bartender!!!"

"She didn't castrate me."

I fold my arms proudly and assume a victory stance. Charles continues his inquiry of Randy.

"You're full of shit, Randy. Why did you wear the corduroy sport coat, then?"

Randy turns to me. "I wore the sport coat because I like you. I wanted you to see this as a date."

A date??!! Does Randy usually invite his date's girlfriend along?? And two of his friends? That's not a date, that's a field trip!

I am just so tired of yelling and crying. Every New Year's, there's some yelling and crying involved. Kids. Me on a stretcher. Me getting verbally attacked by near-strangers during a "New Year's Eve talk." I want to go home. It's 2:15 A.M. and this is another New Year's shot to hell. I ask Abby if she is ready to go. She jumps up and grabs her coat like she's been waiting all night to hear those words. We put on our coats and head into the blustery January air. I'm glad we stopped back by Randy's house to get my car before we came here. And my car actually starts on the first try. That's a good New Year's sign. Abby falls asleep almost as soon as we get into the car. Poor Abby. What a sad New Year's I dragged her into.

No, poor me. Abby got all this entertainment for free. I still have to pay Randy back. I will never speak to him again after I pay him back. His lending me money doesn't mean he can let his friends yell at me.

I still have a lot to learn about castration, emasculation, and sport coats, but I know one thing: I am going to start saving up for next New Year's now. Because Randy lent me the money to join him and his friends, somehow in the world men live in, that gave him the right to call me his date. If he wanted a date, he could have called an escort service. I bet escorts don't even get yelled at like I did tonight.

Having your own money equals freedom. I want to taste New Year's Eve freedom, dammit. Next year, I promise, I'm going to have my own money. No more baby-sitting, corneal abrasions, or screaming matches.

Ang

(Note: In a weird turn of events, Angela later became best of friends with Charles and may offer to mother his love children.

Her friendship with Randy has since dissolved. Moral? Yell a lot and don't wear corduroy. It always gets you the woman.)

---

JANUARY 5

Dear Broke Diary:

I've been standing in line for seven minutes.

Oh, you know which line. It's the beginning of the spring semester and I'm in line.

No, of course I'm not in the bookstore line, I can't afford textbooks.

This is the "sign up for our credit card and get a free gift pack full of toiletries and mints" line.

I'm kinda in a rush today, but Janelle says the cans of shaving cream are really big this year. Plus, she told me they don't have "Not for Sale" stamped on the bottom of the can like the ones last year. That means we can hang on to them until the holidays and give them to relatives as stocking stuffers.

I know I'm a hypocrite. I balk at giving my Social Security number to the phone-company people, but I will not only give my Social Security number to this man with the free Certs, I will wait in line as long as it takes to do so.

I am waiting in line to exchange my personal information for shaving cream, deodorant, and food.

This is my own personal Great Depression.

Oh well, I hope I get spearmint flavor this year.

I don't like peppermint.

Love,

Angie

JANUARY 6

Dear Broke Diary:

You know what? Call me slow, but those mints aren't free.

I'm looking at my last six credit-card statements, and through my interest accrual and late fees I'm subsidizing the free-mint program for every student in North America.

How'd I get used like this? I didn't even mean to use this credit card. Ever. I signed up for it last year, got my free Frisbee, and promised myself it would be only for emergencies. That is, if I was even approved: Why would they give a card to a student who earns less in a year than most people pay in taxes?

Well, obviously if I'm sitting here writing about the card, they approved me. Amazing how things become "emergencies" when you can charge them to a credit card. That new leather jacket, boy, if I ever get stuck somewhere out of town, I'm sure it will transform into a train ticket and get me home. Good old emergency leather jacket.

So, um, if you're a college student reading this right now and you have soft silky legs and cool minty fresh breath, thank me, okay? Don't thank the guy at the credit-card table. He's there to bring you down.

I'm serious. I think I need to go see a campus counselor. I don't think I can walk by that mint table again. If I see a student pop a mint, I might snatch him up by the collar and take the rest of the pack. Those mints are mine! And everyone on campus should be stinky and hairy except for me. Gimme my mints!

Know what? I'm going to get back in that line right now and

get five more packs. I deserve at least that. I'll write down fake Social Security numbers.

*Ang*

Postscript at 4:00 P.M.:

Well, well, well. Don't I feel a tad stupid? I forgot that you had to give the dude at the sign-up table your student I.D. Which, coincidentally, has your Social Security number on it. I couldn't put down a fake Social Security number, so I might be getting two new credit cards. (Whose bright idea was it to put our Social Security numbers on our I.D.s? Lose your I.D. and someone knows what you look like, has your signature, can look in the student directory to get your address, then can sign up for a home mortgage. Hell, with the info that's on our student I.D., someone can steal our whole identity. Go, Ivy League!) (P.P.S. I hear they are going to stop doing that next year. Wonder how many meetings that'll take and if it'll raise tuition.)

---

JANUARY 7

Dear Broke Diary:

I think I may no longer have to commit misdemeanors to make sure I pass my classes.

You remember how Janelle stole that book from our teaching assistant's office last semester, right? Well, she actually felt kind of bad about that, so she's been stealthily searching for ways to get free books that don't involve the "grab and run" technique.

This morning, she called me at 9:15 A.M. I was in no rush to answer the ring, because it could only have been a bill collector at that early hour.

After the fourth ring, I roll over and answer the phone in an overexaggerated sleepy manner.

Janelle's voice starts shrieking through my phone.

"Girl, ohmygod! Wake up! I have just found the book hookup of LIFE!!!"

Janelle's voice is so high-pitched, it's damn near a whistle. Her calling me this early *and* screaming? This must truly be the "book hookup of LIFE." The thought jolts me awake.

I haven't said anything besides my sleepy "Hello" yet; she keeps shrilling on about how "great" and "sweet" the hookup is, but those are only adjectives. I need action words. Verbs. Please. Janelle.

I interrupt her infomercial.

"Janelle. You woke me up to brag? I know you're going to give me details on how to get the book hookup!"

"Come over! I can't tell you over the phone! You owe me big-time for this one!"

Now, I highly doubt that our fine university conducts phone taps on its students (though if they did, I'd surely be the first one bugged), but I agree to get dressed and walk to Janelle's house. She is the monk on the mountain, I am the one seeking knowledge. It is I who must climb.

When I get to her house, I don't even have to ring her doorbell. She's already on her porch, pacing excitedly with a cigarette dangling between her fingertips. She hardly ever smokes. This is all so highly dramatic, it better be good.

As soon as I reach the top step, she hands me a cardboard box. "Read this," she says.

The box has an overnight-shipping sticker on it. I have no idea what this P.O. box is on the return label. It's addressed to Janelle. Well, actually, to Professor Janelle Hall.

"Open it, Ang."

I do.

Wow.

Not only does it contain the main textbook for our psychology class, it also includes a "Guide for Teachers" and a whole 'nother book filled with sample test questions for each chapter. This is too good to be true. Like, this is stuff students aren't supposed to see! How'd she get it sent to her house? And I know she's not about to tell me she didn't pay for this stuff.

Janelle blows a stream of smoke out the side of her mouth, proudly folds her arms, fixes her eyes on mine, and declares, "I got all of this for free. Can you believe how fly this is? I don't think I'll ever pay for another book in my life!"

If she didn't stop showing off and tell me how to do it for my classes, I was set to smack her upside her head with the damn box and knock her off of her own porch. You don't tease a fellow Brokette with tales of free books during the first week of classes and not share your secrets! That's against the code of honor! Lucky for her, she started speaking.

"You know Sue, the psychology secretary, right? I was talking with her about finances and stuff, telling her how hard it was to afford all these books. She starts telling me I need to become a professor, 'cause she opens packages from publishing houses to the professors every day. Sue said if the publishing houses think I'm a professor and I tell them I'm thinking about using their book for a class, they'll send it to me for free."

Well, I'll be damned. The secretaries do know it all, don't they? A lot of students aren't as polite as they should be to the secretaries, but my broke crew is. We actually have people in our families who are secretaries, so we know the deal. It's funny when some students talk about hacking into the Registrar's Office computers to change their grades. Wouldn't it just be easier to establish a rapport with the secretaries who enter the grades? Secretaries rule.

Janelle looks at her watch and says she has to get ready for class. "I'm actually excited about class today," she says. "I have the book."

And, by God, I shall soon have the book as well!

It's 10:20 A.M. now. I'm not going back to sleep. I'm calling Directory Assistance and getting the number for the publisher of every book on each of my syllabi.

I'm already excited, and I haven't even seen one free book yet. Man, if it works for me as smoothly as it worked for Janelle, I'm ordering books for classes I'm not even in. I'll be the campus book dealer.

I'll be the queen of broke students!

*Official secretary groupie,*
*Angie*

---

JANUARY 12

Dear Broke Diary:

Excuse me while I put this pen down and back-flip buck naked off of my couch again! Woohoo!

My first set of books came! Woohoo! Woohoo!

Okay, okay, so I punked out a little: I couldn't proclaim myself a professor on the first call. That just seemed too much of a leap. *Professor Angela Nissel.* Every time I said it aloud to myself I began to chuckle, so I couldn't get up the nerve to say it to a stranger on the phone.

> Me: Yes, I'd like a copy of your book *Introduction to Cultural Anthropology* to review for this upcoming class I'm going to be teaching.
> Them: Sure, and who should we send it to?
> Me: Professor Angela Nuh-nuh-nuh-bwhahahahah!!
> Them: And how do you spell that?

I don't think that would have gotten me a free book. A complimentary copy of *Self-help Psychiatry* perhaps, but that's not the textbook I am looking for.

I reinvented myself as a teaching assistant. A lost teaching assistant who was just trying to follow her professor's orders for getting her free book.

"Hi, I'm trying to get the teacher's edition of *Introduction to*

*Cultural Anthropology.* I'm heading up three recitations this semester and my professor said I should call here."

"Sure, I'll be happy to help you with that. Where should I send the book to?"

I gave her my address, inserting "Department of Anthropology" in front of my street address. I also changed my apartment number to a suite number, just to make it sound a little more authentic.

"Do you need a teaching guide and sample tests also?"

I am surprised she didn't hear me gasp. I'm not only getting free books, they are thrusting additional aids upon me! When I grow up, I want to be a teaching assistant!

"Yes, actually. That would be great. Send those along, too." (I was tryin' all hard to sound proper, I don't know why. . . . The teaching assistants talk worse than I do.)

Today the postman delivered the package right to my door. I was a little nervous signing for it. I always expect some undercover collegiate SWAT team to swoop down on me when I scam for the sake of higher education. But today I sit here, without handcuffs, starting my anthropology reading.

Crime is addictive. I think I'm ready to take it to that next level. For my next book act, I'll gather up my courage and step up to the role of professor.

When I do start my Broke Student Union, I'm going to tell every member about this scam!

Then again, no, I better keep this one to myself. If word of this spreads, someone at the publishing houses is apt to catch on. "University of Pennsylvania sure has a lot of anthropology professors!" Plus, if the rich kids find out, they'll abuse it and use their parents' money to buy more beer.

Today is a wonderful day. My only wish is that it didn't take until the last semester of my senior year to find this out.

Love,

Professor Nuh-nuh-nuh-bwhahahahah (aka Ang)

---

JANUARY 14

Dear Broke Diary:

I made $4,750 last year.

I got a $1,200 phone bill today.

For me, seeing a Total Amount Due of $1,200 is like the guy who makes $50,000 a year getting a $12,500 phone bill.

You with me now? The phone company is telling me I owe it one fourth of a year's salary.

If I'd actually made $1,200 worth of phone calls, I'd live up to my obligations and pay the phone company. No effing sweat. I'd just go without a phone for four or five years while I paid them for the calls, you know? Whatever it took to make up for the stupidity of making $1,200 in phone calls, I'd do. I'd have to because I was dumb enough to make that many phone calls.

Um, okay. I'd lie my ass off at first and act like I didn't make any of the calls. I'd be faking tears and everything. I'd talk about my sick kids, my dying dog, flirt with the customer-service guy. Whatever. You do what you gotta do. That's $1,200.

Then, if they didn't believe me, I'd work out a payment plan. None of this matters, though. This $1,200 phone bill I received is 100 percent phone company error. I don't have to lie because I didn't do anything wrong. (Now, there's a quote of the month for ya!)

Boy, big companies sure will tell a lowly customer when

we've made an error. Let you or me make a mistake and forget to send in payments for a couple of months, they'll send warning letters every day. They'll embarrass us by calling us at work. They will spend $500 to get back the $50 that we owe them. But don't try to tell *them* they've messed something up. It's like the error process doesn't work in reverse.

Even if you somehow miraculously get them to admit they've wronged you, getting them to actually correct it is another matter entirely.

For the past six months, I have been receiving error-filled bills. I've called in and reported the errors every time. No one has yet to correct the problem.

Here's the reason I was given as to why my bills are so high: I am mistakenly being billed the business rate of up to a dollar per minute for long-distance calls.

Linda, the customer-care representative I spoke to last time, says it's because I have a "recycled phone number" that used to belong to a business. A "Pete's Restaurant," to be exact. No one at the phone company pressed whatever button they needed to press to let billing know that this phone number no longer belongs to Pete and his business but to a regular ol' residential customer.

One time, you know, back before my phone company thought I was running a Fortune 500 company out of my efficiency apartment, I didn't pay my long distance for two months and they just cut it off. No note, no calls. Just tried to dial Chicago one day and got a message saying such costly calls weren't allowed from my phone.

Like I said, this is the sixth month this has been going on. (Note to Broke People: You might want to sign up for phone service as a business. It seems that you can dodge your long-distance bill forever and you will never get your service shut off! Your credit will be messed up, but hey, if you're broke, it probably already is!)

Every month, I spend at least an hour on the phone with "customer-care people" trying to get this straightened out. They keep telling me it's fixed, so I start making calls again, but when I get the bill, I'm still being charged the business long-distance rates. I have not paid one of these bogus long-distance bills, and now we're up to $1,200.

They even handed my account over to a collection agency. Like my credit isn't messed up enough already without them adding on stuff that's not even my fault.

While I was opening my phone bill today, I was praying that the phone company had finally come correct. I cannot take another month of this. Six months of having basic phone service shut off every month for nonpayment, only to get them to restore it after I explain the situation, but then they charge me a restoration fee, as if this whole thing wasn't their fault to begin with.

I was steamin' after I opened this bill. I'm still trying to calm down.

I can't. It's been six months. My politeness platter expires after four months. At five months, it smells up the whole house. At six months, it transforms into a emotional delicacy known as GOTDAMN BURNING ANGER. I just have a li'l temper, that's all.

I was going to call the company and curse out every single "phone person," but it's so hard to get a human on the phone on a Saturday. I'd just be cursing into someone's voice mail, and there is nothing that sounds dumber than an angry voice-mail message. Would you call back someone who was flipping out?

I decided to calm down and fax the letter below to the company that has been billing me, to help them understand that I do not own a business.

To: The "Please Give This Girl Her Money Back" Office
COMPANY: LD Discount Plan

Hello to all my friends at LD Discount Plan!

It's me, the girl in Philadelphia who does not own a business but is being billed as one!!

Yeah, hi! How are you? How's your mom? Great, great. That's good.

I'm not so good.

While I am still waiting on credits from your company, I have received (gasp!) yet another bill with these lovely business rates. Imagine calling your aunt in New York to find out what size your cousin wears so you can buy him a sweater for his birthday, only to get the bill for that call and realize you can't afford the sweater anymore and now your cousin thinks you don't care. Why are you breaking apart my family, LD Discount Plan?

Hopefully, after that long three-way call last month with my local carrier, your company, and myself, everyone involved will realize that I am not a business, I am a woman. I am tired of being treated like a McDonald's.

Could I please receive my credit for the last month, as well as the other ones I am entitled to?

C'mon, how would you feel seeing a bill like this, month after month after month?

Hope your New Year's went well. I know you guys so well, maybe I'll be invited to the holiday office party next year!

Sincerely,

Angela Nissel

CEO of Nothing, Nada, Zilch, and Zip, LLC

If you cannot read this fax, please call me. I'm doing it on the computer, when I'm really more of a "take it to Kinko's" kind of gal. I would have my secretary do it, but HEY!, she doesn't exist.

Please call me at least to let me know the amount of my credit. You used to do it every month. Recently, I haven't received a call. I'm beginning to feel so used.

I got a call about ten minutes after I sent this fax. Some lady told me she thought the fax was funny and she'd get to working on the problem right away. The true test will come, of course, when I see a credit on my bill.

Feel free to modify and use this letter to suit your needs if anyone at your phone company happens to think you're a business (yeah, like this would ever happen to anyone besides me . . . ).

Love,

Angie

JANUARY 17

Dear Broke Diary:

My car won't start again. I think it might be dead for good this time.

I hate catching the bus.

Hmm, no, actually being on the bus is okay. It's waiting at the bus stop that I hate.

People who drive by look down their noses at me.

No, I'm not paranoid! I'm serious! If I'm on the corner and a car has stopped at the light or whatever, at least one person in the car will look at me. No smile. Just a condescending stare until they drive off. I hate people who think they are cute because they ride in cars.

I know my bus-stop people feel me. Don't people just stare at you like they're on a bus-stop tour and you're one of the monuments?

"Ladies and gentlemen, if you'd look to your left, you'll see a young lady waiting on the 42 bus. She's only going ten blocks, but it will take her an hour. Actually, ladies and gentlemen, you don't have to look at her too closely, we can go get some refreshments, see the Liberty Bell, and homegirl will still be standing right there when we get back."

Hmm, know what? About five more cars have passed by, and I notice not everyone stares at me. The overwhelming majority of stares come from the eyes of women. Women riding shotgun with a man at the wheel.

They were probably thinking of breaking up with their man, then took a good hard look at shivering little old me and saw a vision of their manless, carless future.

"Damn, I can't break up with Justin yet. It's too damn cold. I'll be at the bus stop, teeth chattering, just like that curly-head girl right there. I'll wait until the spring."

Yeah, it's mostly passenger women giving me that look, but sometimes whole cars of folk will look. Sometimes everyone laughs. I hate that.

Are they laughing at me 'cause I'm doing that street-sidewalk two-step? You know, the one where you walk into the street and crane your neck to see if the bus is coming? It's usually not, so you walk your ass right back to the sidewalk and wait some more. Why do we do that? It's not like most of us have another option if the bus isn't coming. We're catching the bus 'cause we don't have cab money. Duh.

Maybe I'm being paranoid. No one is staring or laughing at me.

Maybe I'm just bitter.

Bitter because going from working car back to the bus stop is, like, the ultimate status drop.

Bitter because there was nothing like just being able to get in my car and actually park near my destination. Nothing like being able to leave someplace whenever I wanted to leave.

Damn, I'm in a bad mood, right? I'm sorry. Bus stop'll do that to you.

I got the bitter bus-stop blues.

Whoa! I'm a genius! I'm going to make a song called "The Bitter Bus-Stop Blues." No instruments except horns interspersed with the "ding ding" of the rope you pull on to signal your stop. The chorus will be people shouting, "Back door!"

Okay, I'm bugging out. Making up bus-stop songs like I work for Sesame Street or something. Maybe I should just go home. This isn't a necessary trip. I'm meeting up with Victoria and going to a cabaret with her and her two cousins.

I do kinda want to go. That's why I'm on this corner in the cold. I've never been to a cabaret. Hell, I don't even know what a cabaret is. What I do know is that this bus better hurry up, because I have to be at her house in twenty minutes.

What else I know is that this chick in the burgundy Buick better stop staring at me before I throw this notepad at her.

*C'mon, bus,*

*Ang*

---

JANUARY 18, 8:03 A.M.

Dear Broke Diary:

Whew! That cabaret was fun!! I'm glad I stayed all night! I'm about to send a thank-you card to Victoria's cousins! Thanks for the tickets, guys! So much fun!

*Love,*

*Ang*

Just kidding.

You know I wouldn't be up this early writing about the cabaret had it actually been a joyous shindig. (Actually, any weekend night I'm not at home fantasizing about all the people who are out having fun isn't a total loss. Just wanted to put that out there in case I sound depressing.)

I'd met Victoria's cousins once before. Gerald and Peanut (no, I have no idea what his real name is). They're the regular guys next door . . . if you live in public housing, that is.

No, I'm not putting them down. They are sweet, polite guys,

just a bit rough around the edges. That's why the thought of going to something as exotic-sounding as a cabaret with them sounded intriguing. Were they hiding some upper-crust mannerisms in their Timberlands? How'd they even get invited to a cabaret? I mean, a cabaret is some high-class French thing, right?

Well, ooh la la, let me tell you something: This wasn't a French cabaret. I mean, unless the French have changed the word to mean "no food and bad band." I don't have a French-English dictionary to tell you if they did, so I'mma just tell you what I now know about cabarets.

Based on my field study last night, cabarets are held in the subbasements of churches. Long, rectangular wooden tables are pushed together by the cabaret-goers to make cabaret tables. You should wear gloves to a cabaret, not those long, elegant gloves that go up to your elbows, but utility gloves. If you try to push a long wooden table without them, you will end up with two cabaret splinters, like I did.

There's nothing wrong with manual labor. Helps you build up an appetite for all the delicious cabaret food.

"Wait, they are serving food, right?"

Victoria asked that after we'd been sitting at our newly constructed table for ten minutes watching all the other cabaretians chowing down.

Gerald surveys the room and replies, "I don't think they're serving food. Everyone else has picnic baskets and paper bags of food."

Victoria looks at him incredulously. "So you guys invited us to a foodless event?"

Peanut folds his arms together on the table, rests his head on top of them, and closes his eyes. Guess he's seen enough family fights to know it's better to go to bed. Even if you are in the middle of a cabaret. Good night, Peanut!

Victoria continues her inquiry. "Well, can you *ask* someone? How are you going to invite us someplace without food??"

"How the hell was I supposed to know they ain't have food? I ain't never been to a cabaret! Pea's mom gave me these tickets. She got 'em from her hairdresser," Gerald replies.

Peanut pops his head up. "Don't bring my mom into this! Like it's her fault we at a bootleg cabaret with no food . . ."

"I didn't say a damn thing about your mom!"

Victoria jumps in before things get too heated. "Why doesn't someone just go ask one of the people who took our ticket if they are serving food?"

Gerald hops up and goes to the door. Peanut plops his head back down on the table. I'm focusing on the band. The lead guy is oversinging an old Earth, Wind & Fire song.

> Take a ride in the skyyyyyyyyy, on a ship
> Fantasiiiiiiiiiiiiii . . .

Nice.

Gerald approaches the table again. What wisdom has he found?

"Everybody, chip in five bucks. I'm going to get some food."

I start laughing. Victoria sucks her teeth. Peanut lifts his head, digs into his wallet, and throws a ten-dollar bill on the table.

I'm still laughing because I have $5, but that's all I have. And

I'm about to give it up to participate in this cabaret. I bet there are fifty meetings happening right now on campus with free pizza. Without bad singers.

I've heard of BYOB, but BYOF? Wait, we have to get our own beverages, too, so I guess this is BYOBandF. This is like paying to get into a buffet that doesn't have any food. Not even a roll. Thing is, the buffet workers are looking at you like you're crazy for expecting there to be some. Yeah, this is like paying to go into an empty museum. The curator explains, "Oh, our museum has a strict 'bring your own exhibit' policy. The entrance price is just for the pleasure of hanging out here."

I can't believe it's legal to sell tickets to a foodless event. What the hell did the entrance price cover? The privilege to eat in the church basement? Homeless people get to do that free every Wednesday! I'll just come back on Wednesday!

Hold up. Everyone is waiting for me to chip in my money. If I'm putting my last $5 in for some food, I want to know exactly what he plans on getting.

"Kentucky Fried Chicken. That's the only thing close by. Well, that and the Stop and Go liquor store." ("Stop and Go" is such a rude name for a store, don't you think? Why are liquor stores in urban areas called that? I'm going to open a classy malt liquor shop one day called "Pause and Enjoy." You just wait. It'll blow up and make me rich!)

Damn, Kentucky Fried Chicken. I wanted to avoid finger food. I might eat my cabaret splinters by accident. Oh well, I guess if that's the only thing open, I have no choice.

Gerald takes our money and heads back to surface level to fetch our extra-crispy cabaret fare. An older lady comes over to our table, gives Victoria a hug, and asks her to meet her son-in-law. I'm left at the table with a still-snoozing Peanut. God, this is embarrassing.

Now, why does Peanut have to make me look like the bad date? No, I don't look like the bad date. If I were a bad date, he'd be looking around bored or would have left me at the table. I'm alert and his head is on the table with his mouth halfway open: He's making me look like I slipped something in his drink. I wish he'd sit the hell up.

Oh well, I can always focus on the band. They're covering Stevie Wonder's greatest hits now. In the exact order in which they appear on Mr. Wonder's *Greatest Hits* album. I bet "Superstition" is next. Oh, it is! Miraculous!

Hey, since when has "Superstition" become a call-and-response song?

"Verrrrrrry superstitious! C'mon, say the next part with me, y'all!"

Everyone is ignoring the singer. Well, except me. Of course, I have nothing else to pay attention to, except the back of Peanut's head.

Oh goodie, the lead singer is now making rounds around the room. Guess he's going to walk around and panhandle for his props, since people weren't exactly throwing them up on the stage. And of course, by accident, I've given him eye contact just as he decided to leave the stage.

Lord, please don't let this man come over here singing. Lord, I'm in the subbasement of your house. I pray you not let this man come over here singing.

Why is he looking over here?

*Please God no.*

Dammit. Peanut, lift your head up and talk to me.

Aw, man, Singer is still looking over here. Where's Victoria? Is she upstairs getting married to that old lady's son-in-law or something? I mean, damn!

Singer is walking this way.

"Verrrrrrry superstitious!"

Eff this!! I plonk my head down on the table just like Peanut.

I know we look crazy. Two people sleeping at an empty table in the middle of a cabaret filled with revelry. I don't care. It's worth the embarrassment to avoid the ridicule of having Singer come to the table crooning "Part-Time Lover" to me.

The double-sleep move worked. I hear Singer belt the end of Stevie's first disc and say he'll be right back after a short break.

Just as he makes that announcement, I lift my head and see Gerald putting a bucket of chicken down on the table. A bucket of chicken and a six-pack of wine coolers. Way to go, Gerald!

Victoria must have smelled the Original Recipe because she came back soon after he set the bucket down. Peanut lifted his head and smiled. Damn, I wish I were as exciting to both of them as this bucket of chicken.

We're finger lickin' as Singer retakes the stage. I guess he was still upset about not getting to embarrass me earlier, 'cause the first thing he does is point to our table.

"Let's give those folks a hand for getting some food! I was thinking that was the sleepy anorexic table!"

Weak joke, dude. I know people are laughing at it, but half of them are drunk anyway.

By the time we plowed through the wine coolers and white meat, the cabaret was winding down. Gerald drove me home, I had a nice buzz, and my stomach was very full.

So, damn. I don't know what I was complaining about at the

beginning of this entry. I got a buzz, food, and a chauffeured ride home for $5.

I guess the cabaret wasn't as bad as I was setting it up to be. All's well that ends well, or whatever they say.

Sorry about that, y'all. I feel like I'm letting this entry down.

Wait, you shouldn't be reading my diary anyway. How are you reading this? Who gave this to you?

*Au revoir,*

*Ang*

---

JANUARY 19

Dear Broke Diary:

I spent my last five dollars on cabaret chicken. I am so broke today I am going to knock out my own tooth and hope the Tooth Fairy is down for adults.

*Ang*

---

JANUARY 24

Dear Broke Diary:

Q: What's almost always free?

A: Open-mike poetry.

Q: That's a bad thing, though. Right?

A: Yes.

Something that's *always* free can't be too good.

I'm back from my first one. Yes, I saw all you broke little ar-teests and college students there, but you know you weren't enjoying yourself. If you had an option, I know you wouldn't be there.

Never been to one? Let me break it down for you:

*Open mike.*

That means anyone from off the street can get up and say something to a roomful of people. At least one performer is going to be crazy. That's the law of statistics, man.

*Poetry.*

The open-mike part is already giving strangers a platform to speak. But to let these strangers recite *poetry*? Poetry can be anything. If someone gets up and says nothing but curse words, is anyone going to tell him to stop? It's poetry, dude. He's just expressing himself! It could be Tourette's syndrome poetry.

Now, what was I saying? Oh yeah, I just got back from my first open-mike poetry session.

Oops! I mean "Free Weekly Celebration of Words" session. That's what the host kept saying.

"Welcome to our Free Weekly Celebration of Words!"

Now, I don't know what kinds of celebrations most people go to, but these poets were way too hostile and angry for something billed as a "celebration." Instead of poetry, they should have put all that energy into protests, petitions, or making picket signs. Something. I don't know what they were telling me their problems for, but I got a kick out of them, so I can't complain.

The first poet set the tone for the entire evening. He must have gotten there really early to be the first person on the sign-up sheet, 'cause me and 'Nelle got there right at the scheduled starting time and every seat was filled up.

So anyway, this first guy goes up to the podium, unhooks the mike from the stand, and starts pacing without saying anything. After about a minute of silent pacing, he stops, faces the audience, bugs out his eyes, and hollers, "YOU'RE NOT READY FOR THE REVOLUTION!" into the microphone.

Then he screams it again.

"YOU'RE NOT READY FOR THE REVOLUTION!"

Oh yeah! Let's see if he says it one more time! Revolution! Yes!

"REVOLUTION!"

Oh wow! This is too exciting! Can we get another "Revolution"?

"REVOLUTION!"

Goodness! This guy is so unpredictable! Poetry, indeed! Will he manage to spurt out another "Revolution"? We can only hope!

Damn. No more straight-up revolution. Instead, he switches to a call-and-response revolution.

"EVERYONE SAY, 'REVOLUTION!' "

No one says a damn thing.

He tries again. Louder.

"EVERYONE SAY, 'REVOLUTION!!' "

Silence.

I kinda felt bad for him, but I was not about to stand in a bookstore screaming, "REVOLUTION!" when I didn't even know what he was revolting against. Try giving us some context next time, bro! Like, I mean, what if he is revolting against women who couldn't care less about a bookstore revolution, and everyone decides to jump me? I'd be a damn fool yelling, "REVOLUTION!" and supporting my own beat-down.

He gives the revolution pitch one more go, except this last time, he held the mike head right in this middle-aged lady's face after he shouted his plea. She looked terrified and peeped out, "Um . . . Revolution!"

I thought I would pee on myself. She had this startled, frightened look on her face like when you're daydreaming and a teacher calls your name to answer a question. Naw, her look was worse. Like one hundred times worse. A crazy, vague revolutionary just screamed and shoved a microphone in her face. After that she was probably too scared to read any of her poems about baking cookies. Or whatever her poem was going to be about. Forest animals. Oprah Winfrey. Her grandkids. Whatever. Poor thing.

Anyway, I think the brother realized his revolution recruitment tactics needed work, 'cause after he scared old sis, he kind of sighed, then mumbled something about how we were "all sleeping" and we'd "better wake up before the war starts" or we'll "all die."

And he left.

Not just the podium, but the whole building. Picked his coat right up off the chair and was out. I thought that was kind of rude. He wanted people to listen to him, but he couldn't wait and check out the other poets? The only thing that kept me from thoroughly enjoying the acts after him was the worry in the back of my mind that he was coming back with a bomb.

Next up was "Love Me for Me" girl.

She did two poems. Both were about how men can't see past her body to "find her soul."

> Love me for me
> Is it just my body you see . . . ?

Thing was, girlfriend's clothes were so tight, and her poetry so very corny, even Janelle and I couldn't see past her body. I would have raised my hand and suggested she try baggy clothes to get past her man dilemma, but then she'd have nothing to write poetry about. Who am I to kill her hobby?

Oh yeah, and if she had so many men chasing her, why is she in here with us on a Saturday night?

Next.

Stepping up to the poetry plate, we have the stuttering poet. Why did Janelle almost make me laugh out loud during this guy's reading? She kept poking me every time he stuttered. Poor guy. He was just nervous. We'd heard him speaking stutter-free earlier. Janelle was messing me up with all that poking. I was trying to write down this dude's verses so I could accurately clown him in this entry. We'll call him "S-s-s-someone Date Me Puh-puhlease."

All of his poems were about how great women are. He compared us to every natural wonder on Earth. We're

> duh-deeper than the Grand Canyon.

Some of us have

> inner buh-buh-beauty like an oyster.

He would speak one line slowly and then speed the next one

up. It was obvious he was doing the acceleration and braking on purpose, but that, combined with the stutter, made him sonically unbearable. It was like being forced to listen to a warped album that keeps skipping.

Okay, I'm tired, so I'm going to write about this last dude and go to bed.

There were other funny people besides this next dude, but he took the cake. And the candles. And then he licked the plate. And threw it at us.

Let me present to you "Misinformed Militant"!!

I won't lie. Misinformed Militant was kinda good-looking. Except he had on this red beret, like he had just come back from Guardian Angels tryouts and forgotten to take it off. His shirt was green and white, paired up with regular old blue jeans, so the red beret really didn't go. He had such a nice face that I was willing to forgive his red Curtis Sliwa mishap.

Until he opened his mouth.

Everything was a damn conspiracy.

Did you know all of our phones are being tapped? Yep, everyone's. Every time we pick up the phone, someone from the government is listening. How do I know? Misinformed Militant said so!

> Can't talk on my phone
> they are listening to me
> to you
> to me
> no privacy
> none
> no.

Deep, huh? I mean, where is the central office for this phone-tap project? And if everyone's phone is tapped, that means there must be just as many tappers as tappees. Can't listen to more than one person at a time, right? Almost everyone in the U.S. uses a phone, so there are a hell of a lot of people on this project. Hmmm. . . . Who taps the tappers? Man, this is too much to think about. Wouldn't it just be easier for the government to put tracking devices in our heads?

Oh, they are. But that's a new project:

> Doctors ordered to put chips in babies' heads
> that's why they don't want you to give birth at home
> you roam
> they will find you.

Wow, that must be one quick operation. They must hide the postoperative scarring under the baby hair! Oh, not all babies have hair! There must be a conspiracy with nonscarring surgery, too!

And now the biggest conspiracy of them all. Janelle is adopted. Her parents are both black, but we found out today she is white. Well, okay, she could be Asian or Native American, but she's not black.

Because the fifth digit of her Social Security number is not even.

That's how the government tracks black people. By the fifth digit on the Social Security number. All black people have even fifth digits. It's true! Misinformed Militant said so! Now I know why Misinformed Militant has that red cap on! His brain has so much knowledge in it, it's overflowing its casing! He's just trying to contain it!

Shhh! Don't tell nobody about the Social Security number thing, though! It's a government secret.

> Two, four, six, eight
> ensures the government keeps
> itself socially secure from you.

Misinformed, I have one question for you.

Listen closely.

Um, why the hell would the government need a secret way to track something so blatantly obvious??!!

Like you'd apply for a job at the phone-tap center and not get hired because your fifth digit was a 6?

Like racist cops pull you over for no reason, you bust out a fake Social Security card, and say, "What's all this hassle for? I'm a damn 3!"

Cop: I'm sorry, sir, you looked like one of those damn 8 boys. I apologize. Drive on.

Misinformed Militant was really upset about the Social Security number conspiracy. He recited those numbers in his poem like we were all morons for not knowing. He had people, including Janelle, whipping out their Social Security cards (you should know it by heart now, people!).

Whoo, boy. That was crazy! People were actually clapping. Cheering him on and everything.

"You tell 'em! You tell 'em about those fifth numbers!"

And I bet, as I'm telling you about the silliness of the Social Security/phone-tap cover-up, there are some people taking Misinformed's words seriously. They probably want to tell their friend about the Social Security number conspiracy but are too scared to pick up the phone, with the tap patrol and all.

Bwahahah. I have to go to sleep.

Good night!

REVOLUTION!

*Cadence,*

*Angie*

---

JANUARY 25

Dear Broke Diary:

I am so inspired by last night's talents, I am going to try my hand at poetry! I just came back from a trip to the corner store, and that outing inspired this poem. Tell me if it's good, and I'll read it next week!

ODE TO MR. STORE OWNER

Mr. Store Owner, why can't you hook me up?
You know I always buy yo' shit, this time I'm short a
    buck.

If I had a car I'd shop somewhere better
Your meat is mad old and the Swiss tastes like cheddar.

You straight-scamming the poor
Don't make no sense

And now you yell at me
For being short twenty cents?

Man, I should tell your wife what you did the other day
Sticking to my butt like your name was Ben-Gay.

I let you get a feel just 'cause you promised free stuff
I walked out yo' store with shrimp and cotton puffs

Chicken, hash browns, Oil of Olay
Now you wanna front 'cause your wife's here today?

I should do the right thing and cut you with my knife—
But yesterday I pawned it for a tire for my bike.

I'd cut up aisle 1 and the aisle with the Pert
Pour olive juice on your fresh silk shirt

'Cause you bought that with your 90-percent profits
Yeah, broke chick on a rampage and yo' ass can't stop it.

One day when I'm clocking loot, crazy paid
And I come to your li'l store, get my eggs off layaway

Don't even look at me, don't try to make me sleep
I may be busted in the pockets, but this chick ain't
    cheap.

[Applause.]
Thank you! Thank you! I'm not worthy!!!!
*Inner buh-buh-beauty like an oyster,*
*Angie*
P.S. REVOLUTION!

---

JANUARY 26

Dear Broke Diary:
    Kim, that vegetarian girl from down the hall, came by to bor-
row a lightbulb.

I don't think anyone ever really borrows a lightbulb. I don't think I'll see my lightbulb again, but that's not the point.

The point is: What is plant food?

While I am digging under the sink trying to find a lightbulb, Kim goes crazy because my only plant is dying.

"Oh my God! The leaves are almost all brown. Don't let it die! Buy some plant food!"

Hello? I live in a basement apartment. It's a *cave*. I get a smidgen of sunlight in here between 7:00 and 7:10 A.M. That's probably the reason for the brown leaves, Captain Save-a-Plant.

I couldn't believe she told me to buy plant food. I barely have enough people food in this joint. Rule of the house: Humans eat before plants.

And what is "plant food"? Plant food is water and dirt. I give my plant those things. Those pellets I think Kim is referring to are a human invention. Plant Doritos, I guess. They are a tool to get us to spend more money. How did plants survive before those plant-food pellets were invented? If we keep buying plant food, next thing you know there will be gourmet plant food, like they have for cats. A "Fancy Feast" to a cat is the piece of juicy burger that fell off your plate, not some processed mush in a can.

Boycott plant food.

The revolution will not be fertilized! (Okay, I'll stop with the REVOLUTION jokes, but trust me, if you were at that poetry reading, you'd still be laughing, too.)

*Ang*

JANUARY 28

Dear Broke Diary:

Isaac Hayes: This one's for you, ladies . . . oooh.

Thanks, Isaac.

Broke Sisters: You have power. Just being a woman gives you a leg up on your broke male counterparts.

Let me share a little story with you. . . .

Yesterday, I got a light knock at my door. I was annoyed because I was in the middle of writing a ten-pager, but I opened it anyway.

The building security guard and some other dude were standing in my doorway.

Security: "We've got a little problem. . . ."

Well, damn! I bet we do! Building security never leaves the post unless it's some serious shit! And look, the other dude has some type of I.D. badge and uniform, too!

My brain: Run, girlfriend! Run! It's the postal police! They know you've been mailing stuff without a stamp by putting *your* address as the addressee and putting the *real* addressee as the return address! Your abuse of the "Return to Sender, Missing Postage" feature has been found out! Grab your typewriter, your cat, a couple bras, and GO!!

". . . this guy here is turning off your electricity."

I look up. Sure enough, the other guy's blue uniform has the name of the city's electric company sewn across the chest pocket.

My brain: Quick! Stall him while I think of something more effective!

Me: "I just got off the phone with the electric company. Can you call into the base to make *sure* I'm supposed to be cut off?"

Electric Man speaks. "I'm sorry, but I just did that and they told me the account needs to be shut down."

Oooh, he's trying to be slick. But, alas, resistance is futile!

[Insert maniacal laughter here.]

I attempt a retort. "Well, I'm going to have to call the police if you try to come in here and turn my electricity off. . . ."

Yeah, Ang. Great comeback. And like I'm really going to call the police, with this illegal cable hookup I got in here.

He replies, "I don't need to come in to turn it off. I can do it at the main switch."

Ow! Touché!

Security: "Well, I'm going to let you two sort this out. I'll be at my post."

As soon as the security guard is out of sight, Electric Man asks, "What's your ethnicity?"

Hmmm, he is interested in me for some reason. Work with that.

I reply: "I am the offspring of sharecroppers."

Psych! Naw, I tell him my background and add on a few more oppressed races for added effect. The back of my mind is still working on how to keep my hot water on and my electric stove cookin'.

After we climb my family tree a bit, he decides to call into base, "just to make sure" that my service should be shut off! Two points for me.

The base people give him mad hassle and put him on hold. He looks frustrated. While he is on hold, my mind goes back to my bill. I know if you have medical problems, they cannot shut your gas off. I am a medical anthropology major, I know more obscure illnesses than an exotic hypochondriac.

He hangs up his little walkie-talkie. He tells me that yes, my service is to be cut off today. He also says if it were up to him, he wouldn't shut it off.

Oh wow! Sympathy points! Now time to go in for da kill. . . .

I say sweetly and demurely, "But you can't turn my gas off— I have shinkeishitsu [Japanese obsessive-compulsive neurosis]!"

Now, before you start thinking I'm lying, I did have a valid reason for not paying my bill: I'm broke! And who's to say I'm *not* obsessive-compulsive? I'm *obsessed* with graduating, so it's *compulsory* that I finish this paper. I can't do that without electricity.

Electric Man: "So you need electric?"

I feel it, I got him. "Yes, I have an electric stove and I need hot water to boil my chamomile and sassafras. Tea is the only known curing agent for shinkeishitsu."

He smiles and goes to the truck to get some form I need to fill out. When he comes back he tries to fill out the form outside of my doorway by leaning the paper on his knee. I invite him in so he can fill it out on the table.

To make a long story short, he tells me he wasn't going to cut me off no matter what the "base" said. He says I was "too cute" (actually, I was looking busted. No need to do my hair to sit in front of a computer!) and had a "nice disposition." Not only that, he tells me how to get my bill down to zero without paying. He looks up from filling out the form and says, "Wow, I've never done this before."

I tell him this is my first time, too. Just wanted to make him feel special.

He keeps talking. He asks if I could tell he was trying to hit on me when he asked my ethnicity. He tells me he's Russian. Well, he basically tells me his whole life story. Now, get this: He also asks if he could bring me breakfast tomorrow.

"Sure!" I reply. He could drop off some grits for me, for sure! He gives me the form, tells me to stay sweet, then leaves.

This morning, the security guard calls me and says, "That electric guy just dropped off some Denny's for you."

WHAT'S

MY

NAME?

You think I'm lying about all this? Ask my girl Carmen. I called her up after he told me he was Russian, because she majored in Russian. She conversed with Electric Man in his native tongue.

Moral: Broke sisters, don't dis our blue-collar brothers! They have power in the areas of brokeness. Yes, you could try to date the CEO of your utility company, but he actually cares about his job and might not risk giving you the electricity hookup. The people on the bottom rung of the corporate ladder sometimes have more power than the people at the top.

Don't go after a man for cash. That's a temporary fix to your broke problem. Not to mention you'll ruin your rep and your self-esteem. Plus, do you know how much of his bull you'll have to put up with if you have to hang on to him for money? Might as well get another part-time job!

Just be cool, keep a sunny disposition and a smile, and good things will come to you (keeping yourself up physically doesn't hurt; keep your 'fro tight, go to the thrift stores in rich neighborhoods and get your wardrobe on). Men encounter numerous disses in a day; be the one woman who smiles and gives him the time of day—you never know what could happen. You could keep your electricity on like me! Woohoo!

Yeah, it's a messed-up sexist world. You can complain or you can get yours in the form of jobs, degrees, and free utilities.

You can complain or you can use what you got to get what you want.*

You can complain or you can be eating a free Denny's breakfast platter with raspberry ice tea with your electricity on while you write your final paper for Human Biology.

*Pass the syrup,*

*Angie*

---

*I'm talking about your mind! Better to have no heat or lights than to be known as the Utility Company Ho!

---

FEBRUARY 2 5:00 A.M.

Dear Broke Diary:

Look at the time: 5:00 A.M. So far, I have gotten twelve minutes of sleep. I stayed up to finish a paper and fell asleep at about 3:30 A.M.

At 3:42 A.M., I am awakened by my cat pouncing on the bed, then darting across my chest. Suddenly my apartment has become a high-speed cat obstacle course. My cat is going crazy! He's running over and under everything. What the hell is wrong with him?

Oh, I see.

*Great.*

He is chasing a freakin' mouse!

Well, at least if I have a mouse I have a cat who will kill it. But *noooooooo*, he wants to *play* with the mouse. He is using his teeth to pick up the mouse by its tail, then he twirls it in the air like a lasso and whirls it up against the wall. When the mouse hits the carpet again, my cat chases it until he gets it in his mouth again and continues with his feline version of wall ball.

Now, I live in an efficiency, so it's not like I can just go into the other room and let him terrorize the mouse in this one. There is no other room. So I just stand up on the bed/couch and yelp every time he throws the mouse near me.

No, it's not *just* a mouse. Who knows where this mouse came from? It could have a disease. I like my mice nice and clean, like Mickey. Mickey Mouse wears clean white gloves. This is a West Philly ghetto mouse. The kind of mouse that Mom Mouse sees standing on the corner and tells her kids to lock their car doors.

I'm trying not to scream too loud, but I must have been louder than I thought, 'cause eventually the security guard figures he'd better check on me. He's here to protect us students!!

What does he do? He grabs my broom and tries to shoo the mouse out of the door. Well, that's what he *said* he was doing.

He sure was shooing the wrong way, 'cause the mouse ran right under my bed. He then shrugs, tells me to "get a shoe box ta catch 'im in," and leaves.

Thanks, pal.

Mouse under bed. Cat can't fit under there. Cat is trippin'

out 'cause he smells the mouse and can't get at him. Cat's eyes are all bugged out. He's making little snort noises with his nose. I lift up my futon so cat can get to mouse. He grabs it and begins this whole "mouse as toy" thing again.

This time, while he's chasing the mouse, it runs into my damn schoolbag! I can't believe it. I can't use that schoolbag anymore! The mouse might have been bleeding, and plus, who knows if he used my backpack as a mouse Porta Potti?

This can't get any worse. I can't afford a new backpack.

Cat, who has no mouse training (he's a big fat house cat), can't find mouse in bag. I am too chickenpoo to pick up the bag and throw it outside. Plus, my books are in there.

Argh.

I place cat inside of the bag and he finds the mouse. I escort bagged mouse and cat into the hallway where the guard sits. He's so good with mice, let him deal with it.

My cat's back home, if anyone cares, but I am too pumped off adrenaline to go to sleep.

*Goofy,*

*Angie*

---

FEBRUARY 7

Dear Broke Diary:

My brother fixed my car (for the fifth time in three months) last night! I'm rolling again! I'm rolling with extremely expired inspection stickers and a fake insurance card, but I'm rolling!

I just have one question:

Um, did you know you're not supposed to cut your car off

after you get a jump if you want it to start again? I guess that's one of those lessons you learn through experience, huh?

I thought an engine is, like, the car equivalent of a heart. It stops, a doctor gets it pumping again, you thank him, get off the operating table, and walk away with your heart pumping just like before. It's like the heart was never even broken, right?

My car's heart was resuscitated at 8:32 A.M. I flatlined it again at 8:50 A.M.

It's now 8:54 A.M., and like the brilliant college student I am, I'm sitting in the same spot in front of the same drugstore in the same broken-down car about to call the same emergency road-service number from the same pay phone.

I feel so damn dumb.

It is so cold, I'm going to keep writing this until my fingers warm up and I get the nerve to call the emergency road-service hotline again.

Yes, I'd rather deal with this little bit of frostbite than be embarrassed if I get the same operator and crazy tow-truck driver again. He kept yelling at me. I don't want to be yelled at again.

He attached his little battery jumper-pack thing to my battery and that's when the yelling started.

"Crank it!"

I turned the ignition key once.

"Crank it again! You don't stop cranking! Just keep cranking!"

Dude, you're under the hood with motors, sparks, and oils and shit. I'm trying not to make sudden ignition moves. I'm trying to be courteous and avoid something like, I dunno, setting your face on fire?

"Crank it!!!"

It's now 8:57 A.M. I'm going to call back at 9:00 A.M. Hopefully, there will be a shift change and I won't get the Screaming Service Man.

I feel like writing a whole bunch of curse words, but so I can share this important lesson with my children later in life, I'll try to refrain from profanity. I'm going to document how this all happened and give it to them when they are old enough to drive. Obviously, someone forgot the "car-jump lecture" when I was younger, and I don't want my future kids to go through the same embarrassment.

(Okay, I'm not writing this to share with any future kids. I'm writing this to keep warm and stall from calling. Just pay attention anyway.)

I've been reading a lot of self-help books lately 'cause, dammit, I need help. One of the books is really good. It's got all these time-management tips. This particular Sunday morning, I'm trying to live Lesson 3: Run Your Errands at Off-Peak Hours.

When my car wouldn't start after the first errand, I wasn't upset. As many times as this old thing has died, I just say, "Thanks, car," when she chooses to conk out anyplace other than a highway or bridge.

I'm becoming so used to my car breaking down that it's routine. I don't get sad when she breaks down, I just get happy when she starts. It's the starting part that's unexpected.

So yeah, like any other time my car conks out, I just walked to the pay phone and told the woman who answered the emergency line that I needed a tow. That's what I always need when it doesn't start. My car scoffs at your temporary fixes like tire inflators and spark plugs. She's not one of your punk, sensitive, modern cars. When she dies, she goes hard.

Screaming Service Man, although it took him an hour to get to me, was one good emergency car fixer. He insisted on trying a jump first. And it worked!

Amazing! I thanked him profusely and shut the car off while I ran in to buy the one thing I forgot.

Horrible! My car wouldn't start. Again. And Screaming Service Man was gone.

And I'm still here.

In the same spot.

And right now, I'm going to get out of this cold car, walk bravely towards the pay phone, and get another jump.

I can deal with whatever sarcastic remarks or incredulous looks come my way.

Yep, I'm getting out of this here car and walking towards the pay phone.

After I write one more line so I can stall some more.

Just like my car. Heh.

Okay, I'm going.

*Cranky,*

*Angie*

---

FEBRUARY 15

Dear Broke Diary:

Fred is dead.

I just got off the phone with Andrea. She was remarkably calm as she gave me the news of his departure. I thought she'd be moaning, passing out, and all that mess. She wasn't even sniffling. I'm surprised she even called me to tell me. Our friendship kinda dissolved once she started letting Fred take over her mind.

I remember the day Fred came into her life. Andrea was acting like Psycho Girl that day. I wonder what has happened since then for her to be so nonchalant about his death?

Hmm. I guess I should introduce you to Andrea. My friend Michelle, too. Only after you meet them can you fully understand Fred's birth and the havoc that it caused.

My friend Carmen (last seen speaking Russian to Electric Man) recently remarked, "You have a lot of friends I've never met."

It's true. I mostly enjoy my friends one at a time because they each have quirks I love, but I know all these quirks don't necessarily mix well together. I love peanut butter and I love pickles, but I would never try to mix the two together and think the mix was going to be just as enjoyable as the solitary items.

Andrea is peanut butter. Michelle is pickles.

The day Fred arrived was the first time Michelle and Andrea met. That day proved my Quirk Mixing Theory to be 100 percent accurate.

(Why do I feel like I should be a guest on a talk show?

"Mixing quirks is wrong."

"You might think mixing quirks is wrong, but you have no right to teach your children such close-mindedness!!" [The audience claps.])

Andrea: I met her during my *Dateline* NBC internship last summer. She wasn't an intern, she was dating one of the associate producers. We hit it off right away. She lived in Brooklyn and had a car. A very old car, but a car still. That made her even cooler because almost no one in NYC owns a car. Never met any of her family. She's far from rich, but she's always practicing for her rich debut by using big words and saving up to buy designer labels. Her true socioeconomic status sometimes shines through her practiced polished veneer, though. Especially when she's at a restaurant. She doesn't know that the upper class doesn't usually pair filet mignon with malt liquor. Sometimes she can be a little snooty, 'cause I guess that's what she thinks rich people do. I think it's funny. Maybe if I lived closer to her and had to deal with it every day, it wouldn't be as funny.

Michelle: Known her for ten years. Longer than any of my other friends.

Michelle grew up in the projects and went to college for one semester after we graduated high school. After leaving college, she enrolled in hair school. After a few weeks of styling wigs, Michelle decided that she was not the next Ms. Clairol. She left school, had a baby, and took a secretarial job. Funny thing is, that semester of college she has under her belt is all that matters to a lot of people. It's stuck to her forever. College made her "the smart one" in her neighborhood. Michelle could mess up on the *Soul Train* scramble board and she'd still be a genius in a lot of neighborhood people's eyes:

> Wife: Tom, I can't get the VCR to come on. Come take a look
> at it for me?
> Husband: I don't know nothing about VCRs! Call Michelle!
> You know she went to college for a semester!

Never mind that Michelle only took psychology courses during her twelve-week college career. She knows everything.

Enough introduction. Let's move right along into our story.

On that fateful Freddy day, Andrea was in Philly for some reason and stopped by my apartment unexpectedly. She was driving out to Reading to do some outlet shopping and wanted to know if I wanted to ride along. A nice Sunday drive was more interesting than my Nutritional Anthropology paper, so I agreed to join her on the outlet excursion. Michelle called as I was putting on my coat.

I shouldn't have told Michelle I was on my way out the door, I love Michelle like a sister, but whenever you tell a person *without a car* you're going somewhere *in a car*—they want to go, too. They don't care where. Carless people just like to be in cars.

Michelle: "Ooh! Reading! Come get me! I want to go, too!"

I tell Michelle to hold on, and place my hand over the mouthpiece of the phone as I ask Andrea's permission. Andrea agrees to Michelle joining us. I immediately start getting nervous. It's doubtful that Michelle and Andrea will get along. I just hope for the best as I turn the key to lock my building's front door.

When I turn around to face the street, I am surprised to see Andrea's white 1974 Ford Granada parked at the end of the block. I dunno, I just thought it would have been in a junkyard by now. I certainly didn't think it could make a New York–to–Philly trip.

I guess she saw me looking in semi-amazement, because she interrupted my silent car-doubting analysis with the reminder that her brother is a mechanic and keeps the ride in tip-top shape for her. Oh yeah! I forgot about that.

Her bro might know his way around under the hood, but he's obviously no auto-body specialist. Her Granada has the dullest white finish on earth. It's like a big piece of chalk with windows and wheels. There is a long silver dent running the length of both passenger-side doors. The dent is a perfectly straight line, like someone held a ruler up to the car and carved it in.

The inside of the car is in perfect contrast to the outside. It feels like a home. A very burgundy minihome. Andrea has thoroughly decorated the interior. The carpets are crimson and the air smells like roses. There are brass drink holders and a tiny trash can in the backseat. The glove compartment is really a mini–convenience store, as it contains an overflowing supply of gum, candy, headache medicine, and tissues. Though, if I remember correctly, Andrea doesn't let people eat in her car.

Of course, what the car looks like on the outside and the inside matters none. Andrea has a car that runs. She is on a plane slightly higher than Michelle and myself.

We start driving to pick Michelle up and have a pretty bland conversation about, well, what's wrong with Andrea's life. She's broken up with her boyfriend, she can't seem to jump-start her singing career in NYC (I didn't even know she could sing), and well, she's pretty broke. (But yet she had enough money to fill up her tank and get to Philly and now we're going outlet shopping! Hey! That's not broke!) I want to say that to her, but she is actually pretty sad about her life, so I save her the "you've been rejected by my elitist broke society" speech.

We get to Michelle's house, and when she jumps in the car, Andrea stops talking about her life to introduce herself. Actually, the subject of Andrea's life doesn't come up again. We spend the rest of the forty-five-minute trip to Reading talking about the two things women who have almost nothing in common talk about: 1) men; and 2) boosting our self-esteem by putting down stars who have had plastic surgery.

Wow, that sounds shallow, but really, if I'd talked about my Comprehensive Evolutionary Theory paper, I'd have been kicked out of the car. If Michelle started talking about how her breasts have changed since the baby was born, Andrea and I would have been grossed out and reached for our birth-control pills.

The fun in the car carried over into the outlet stores. Michelle and I shopped vicariously through Andrea. (She spent $90 on clothes. That's way above the broke limit.) There were no fights, thank goodness. Just Andrea shopping and us watching. Shopping as spectator sport.

Once the sun starting setting, we decided to head back to the car and start on the highway home.

When we get to the car, Andrea pops the trunk and sighs, "This car has served me well, I bet it's on its last leg."

Michelle replies loudly, "Oh, this Fred ain't going nowhere. The engine sounds better than my uncle's old car. Don't jinx us and say bad things about Fred's health. Let him get us home. Thanks, Fred, for getting us here!" After her speech, Michelle pats the car's hood lovingly.

Wait. Hold up. *Fred?* Michelle has named Andrea's car? Or can she not pronounce "Ford"?

Andrea and I look at each other quizzically, then we turn our gazes towards Michelle.

With slight hesitation in her voice, Andrea asks, "May I ask why on earth you are calling my car 'Fred'?"

Michelle points to the letters on the car's trunk. "See, F-R-D.

Your O fell off. It's not a Ford anymore, it's a Fred! My uncle's O fell off his old Mustang. Must be something about the glue they use on the O's. . . ."

Michelle's right. There is no more O. Just two rusty sockets where the O used to hang.

Andrea looks down at the spot where her car's only vowel used to live.

Then she snaps.

"Oh, my O! Where's my fucking O? Now the car looks horrible! I don't want a fucking 'Fred' car!! We must find this O!"

As if Michelle renaming the car "Fred" because of a missing O wasn't comic relief enough, now Andrea is running around screaming, "Oh, my O!"

She's joking, right?

Nope.

"Oh, my lost O!"

I wanna laugh.

God, make it stop.

Please, God.

She's still flipping out, but she tries to compose herself and make a definite O plan.

"Okay. Let's strategize, girls. Do y'all remember when I hit the curb a bit when we were turning onto the expressway after we left Michelle's house? I bet it popped off when I hit that curb! Come on! Let's all get in the car so we can get back there and look for it! Damn, Michelle. If only I hadn't stopped to pick you up."

Oh no. Why'd Andrea have to go there? Michelle didn't do anything to make her say that. Andrea really doesn't know Michelle well enough to start a beef with her.

Please don't hit her, Michelle. Let's allow Andrea her little bit of drama so we can get home. She's the driver, so she's in control until we get near home.

Michelle doesn't say anything. She's never had a car, so she's used to the "driver in control" rule. I'd forgotten how smart she is. Michelle went to college, you know.

Even though Michelle was silent, loud waves of tension were bouncing off all that burgundy interior on the way home. Not one word was spoken until we got back to that expressway entrance near Michelle's house.

Andrea drives halfway down the on-ramp, flicks on her blinkers, then actually gets out and leaps into the grass along the side of the ramp. "C'mon, girls. It has got to be here somewhere."

This chick is dead serious. She bends over and starts searching through the grass.

We are in Michelle's rough-ass neighborhood with out-of-state plates searching through grass on the side of a highway entrance. Yes, *we*. Gotta do what you gotta do. I don't have enough money to get home unless Andrea takes me, and she is not leaving this on-ramp until she is satisfied. Let's find this O.

Michelle's facial expression says she's not down for this search mission. Well, that and the fact that she is still sitting in Fred's backseat. Hell, her ass is only a few blocks from home, she can afford not to be down. She is, however, cheering us on:

"Y'all going to get robbed! People are going to think we're looking for our drug stash or something! Stop trippin' and get in the car and buy another gotdamn O!!! Let's go!"

Andrea yells back, "No!"

Wow! Even more comedy! I wanna say a rhyming O sentence, too! "Andrea!" I yell. "Girl, there are oodles of O's! Can't you get one from your bro?"

I look back at Michelle to see if she heard me and has caught on to the potential comedy involved with the O sound. She obviously has, 'cause she's cracking up. The roar of cars whizzing by must have blocked the sound of her laughter, because Andrea would have been furious if she heard it.

Michelle obviously thinks the idea of Andrea getting furious is funny. We *are* in Michelle's neighborhood, and Andrea *did* insult Michelle earlier. I'm siding with Michelle. Let's keep the O jokes coming.

> Michelle: C'mon, Ang. I got money, let's go! I gotta pick up my daughter at fo'!
> Me: Hey, Michelle, walk slow!
> Michelle: I'll walk you to the bus stop! It's near the sto'!

Andrea heard us. She looks pissed now. She knows we're making fun of her. Too bad. I really don't care at this point. Oh shit, my turn to O.

> Me: I only have a dollar, can you get me some mo'?
> Michelle: Yeah, if my mom don't have it, I'll ask Vic or Joe. I'm not trying to look for this O no mo'!

Damn, Michelle's good. She should come to open-mike poetry night with me.

We walk up the ramp together.

Yes, we left Andrea there.

(Yes, I felt kinda bad that I had to go.)

(But eff dying on ramp with Girl Psycho.)

Ang

Dear Broke Diary:

I have some confessions to make.

Let's call 'em "Confessions of a Broke Club-Hopping Sister."

1. *I wear the same tight, shiny black pants to the nightclub every time I go.*

I know my girlfriends have noticed.

They don't call and ask, "What are you wearing to the club tonight?"

They ask, "What top are you wearing with your tight black pants to the club tonight?"

2. *I have worn two different-colored socks to a club.*

Trouser socks are expensive. When the dryer eats one of my socks, I can't just throw the mate away.

I have standards, though. I'd never pair a green and a black sock, but brown, gray, and black are all interchangeable colors. No one in the club can tell if one of my trouser socks is brown and the other is black.

Especially when I have on my black pants and ankle-high boots.

I have never worn *dirty* socks to a club, however.

I think.

Well, I try not to.

3. *Die, Coffee, Die.*

None of this matters since I'm thinking about not going to clubs anymore. Even if they are free before 10:00 P.M.

No, not because I'm embarrassed that I can only afford to buy one pair of club pants, but because women's lib messed it up for all broke sisters.

What's up with the surge of cheap, Frappuccino-drinking men?

If one more guy asks me out on a "coffee date," I will throw my glass of watered-down club drink up against the wall and scream, "That drink cost more than a cup of coffee. The gas it will take to meet you at the coffeehouse will cost more than the coffee. I will have one-upped your coffee and not even gotten to the coffeehouse yet!!! Up your ante!!! Eff a coffee!!"

Then I will sit down and act like I didn't just throw a drink and scream at him.

My friend Carl tells me guys ask women out for coffee because dinner seems like too much of a commitment. "It's easier to get a woman to go out for coffee, because coffee is so casual. It's a drink as opposed to an entrée," explains Carl. "Entrée screams 'commitment.' "

Well, my entrée-fearing brothers, let me clue you in on

something: Let an entrée scream at me, I don't mind. I need a return on my initial club-pants investment and the cheap coffee offers are dripping in a little too frequently.

If a woman has a full-time job, ask her out for coffee. If she's in school, scream entrée all the way, okay?

Job = coffee. School = dinner. Got it?

Good.

I'll be quizzing several of you next weekend.

Just look for the girl in the black pants.

*Starbucks will survive,*

*Angie*

---

FEBRUARY 22

Dear Broke Diary:

My toilet got really sick today and I blamed brokeness for the illness. Turns out it wasn't really brokeness's fault. Hmm, maybe it was, indirectly. Whatever, I'll just tell the story and let you decide. Actually, you don't have to decide anything. No one should ponder toilet bowls for too long. Just listen. Thanks.

I have no alarm clock, so whenever I have to wake up early I drink lots and lots of water before I go to bed. You can ignore an alarm clock, but you can't sleep through a gallon of water climbing through your bladder! I think I drank too much, because all night I was running to the commode.

At around noon today, I get a knock on the door. I open it to see a distressed-looking maintenance man.

"I need to send some guys in to look at your toilet. That okay?"

Damn, did I break it by overflushing? I agree to the commode check, and in come three big men. With big machines. And big frowns.

"Have you been having toilet troubles?" the largest one inquires.

"No."

"We need to remove your toilet. Do you have someplace else you can pee?"

Damn. . . . Um, no, but I'm open to suggestions.

The potbellied bro of the bunch starts taking my toilet out of the ground, and what came up through the pipes once he did that, I won't terrorize you with a description of. Let's just say, my bathroom floor was a great shade of amber.

Which flowed over onto my efficiency's carpet.

I couldn't stand the sight of it, so I went to the library to study (and wash up) in the third-floor bathroom sink. You can't shower with men in your bathroom! Well, okay, you can, but these guys weren't sexy.

2:00 P.M.: I come home. No commode, and the three men are still here. I go back out.

9:00 P.M.: I have just gotten back from aerobics. I am sweaty, rank, and just wanna take a shower, but there are now *four* men crowded around my bathroom door. This is the largest gathering of people I have ever had in my apartment.

I ask if they've found the problem yet. If they say no, I will reveal that I was Queen-o-Flush all night long. Maybe that will help them get to the bottom of it.

The new fourth member, who is sticking something into the hole in the floor where my toilet used to be, hollers, "Yeah, someone stuck a whole mess of feminine products down the toilet!"

Not me! I just moved in! Haven't even been here a full cycle yet!

But, alas alack, what can you do or say when four men are looking at you like "I am supposed to be home drinking beer, but I am here battling Kotex. . . ."

"It wasn't me, y'all."

"Oh, we know. Seems like it came down from the fourth floor and finally made its way here. Since you live on the ground floor by the main plumbing system, it backed up all the way to your bowl. Every time someone backs up their toilet, if they don't report it in time, you're gonna get the brunt of their waste. Fricking feminine products. I hate them."

I am so embarrassed by now. I mean I *didn't* do it, but I'm sitting with four strange men in my crib talking about tampons!

I insert some wit and reply, "Yeah, feminine products . . . the demise of civilization."

They laugh.

I have bonded with the maintenance guys.

11:00 P.M.: Now it's just me and two guys. One is reinstalling my toilet, one is cleaning the carpet with a wet-dry vac. Still don't know when I can pee. If I was a guy, I'd just aim out of the window. But I'm a woman, we have to sit to pee . . . and we clog toilets.

Broke moral: Splurge on an alarm clock and never rent the cheap ground-floor apartment with the plumbing system as the next-door neighbor.

*Pipe dreams,*

*Ang*

---

FEBRUARY 27

Dear Broke Diary:

Despite our years as professional broke asses, I can't believe my friends and I just discovered the Philly weekly paper's "Free Events" listings two days ago.

Before that, we actually *bought* two paperback books on frugal entertainment, thinking that we'd recoup the costs of the books through their helpful money-saving hints.

Well, if the books had given us some *real* money-saving entertainment tips, we'd have recouped. Like how to sneak into the movies without getting caught. Or how to run out of a five-star restaurant without paying.

But *nooooo*, their secret tips were dumb stuff like:

Spend a day in the park instead of a day at the mall.

Stupid. Going to the park instead of the mall isn't a secret tip. One, if it's hot outside and you don't have air-conditioning, you take your ass to the mall and suck up their free cool air.

Two, if it's cold outside, you still don't sit in a park. You go to a mall to suck up their free heat.

Three, we tried that "spend a day in the park" thing freshman year. Each one of my friends ended up almost giving her phone number to random homeless guys. We like those struggling-artist types, and they wear the same clothes homeless guys do. Dirty sneaks. Knotty hair. Beards. It's too easy for a homeless guy to act like he's an eclectic art-school student hanging out in the park. They just hide their shopping carts behind a big park bush and start scheming on you. So, eff a park. Get me to a mall for some climate-controlled window-shopping!

Then again, even window-shopping is beginning to take its toll. My crew and I have been doing it for over three years now and we're beginning to burn out. At first it was fun, but eventually it just depressed us and made us feel even poorer. We'd analyze items not in terms of dollars, but in terms of "How many hours would I have to work to buy this item?"

Most items don't survive this cost-analysis test even if we imagine ourselves having midlevel income. I mean, are new sneakers really worth four hours of work?

Plus, window-shopping was made for malls. We found ourselves window-shopping and doing the work-hours cost analysis in a supermarket once, and by the third aisle we were so hungry and depressed, we were ready to throw ourselves in the meat grinder and end it all.

That was Janelle's fault. She stopped in the cereal aisle, held up a box of Frosted Flakes, pointed to the orange price sticker on the shelf, and exclaimed, "We would have to work over an hour to afford this box of Frosted Flakes and a half gallon of milk!!"

That was a scary moment of clarity right there, boy. If someone said, "Pssst. Work ninety minutes in this cramped office and I'll give you a box of Frosted Flakes and a half gallon of milk," I'd surely not do it. But I do it every day.

*Whoa.*

Scary.

So, um, I can't really recommend window-shopping. Especially if you're prone to thinking about things like how many hours you have to work to afford food staples like Frosted Flakes. The Man doesn't want you thinking about that! Revolution!

Oh, back to these free events. Free events can teach you things. See, I learned about The Man and revolution at that free poetry event I told you about before.

My mom was so unimpressed by my tales of that poetry event. "You want to know about The Man and revolution, you could have come over my house. I was around in the sixties and seventies!" Yeah, that's true, but I don't want to go back to my mom's house until she gets touch-tone dialing. Dialing that damn rotary phone made me break a nail last time I was over there. She needs a phone revolution.

Anyway, what was I talking about again? Oh, the free stuff we found in the weekly paper. *Free events listed in a free weekly paper.* That's, like, a double free! I think every major city has at least one free weekly paper. It's usually billed as the "alternative paper." If you're not sure if it's the right paper, look at the back pages. If it has ads back there for transsexual escorts and phone dating services, you've got the right paper.

Finding those free events was an eye-opener. We'd been missing out on a plethora of free! Hmmm, I think The Man wants broke people to miss out on the free events. Why else is there a newspaper box overflowing with free-event listings found on every corner only in the rich downtown neighborhoods? Give the free events to the kids in public housing!

Oh well, can't worry about working for social justice right now. Too many free events to get ready to go to.

The most plentiful free event in these weekly papers seems to be poetry readings. I've already given you the lowdown on free poetry readings. I'm sure the ones in this paper aren't any different from the one me and Janelle went to.

All broke people should definitely give one of those a go. If for no other reason than to laugh at other people and be very thankful for whatever crazy life you have.

Besides the poetry readings, I see lots of listings for free lectures. I'm not really too keen on that. I mean, we pay all this money for college, and half of these lectures are "please someone hit me in the head with a rock and end this pain" boring, so you imagine how bad a free lecture would be. Unpaid lecturers can't be happy people, so I bet they use their forums to transfer their anguish to the audience.

You want a free lecture? Call your mom and tell her you're out of money again.

Nope, I retract that. The only thing better than a free lecture is a lecture you get paid to listen to. Go to work and mess up a big project. Nothing big enough to get fired, of course. While your supervisor is lecturing you about responsibility, watch the clock and calculate how much she is paying you to listen to her.

Well, besides the poetry and the readings, the only other events listed in abundance are nature walks. Janelle and I have decided this will be the next one we hit up. The listing says to bring waterproof boots, and I already have those, so I'm fully prepared. I'll write back and let you know how it goes.

I have to run out and get a Sunday paper now. I like to cut

coupons, and the free weekly papers don't have any. Getting those Sunday-paper coupons is a must. With all these stores offering double coupons, I end up working seventy-five minutes instead of ninety for my Frosted Flakes. Can't beat that!

*Coupons: They're grrrreat!*

*Ang*

---

## MARCH 3

Dear Broke Diary:

My umbrella broke today.

It was one of those cheap ones, but it was really cool 'cause it had the automatic button thingie. It was kinda already broken, because when you pressed the button, if you didn't hold on to the shaft (yikes, is that the right word??) of the umbrella, the top half would shoot off and become a deadly projectile!

I know it's unsafe, but you should see the look people give me when it hits them! It's worth every eye I put out! Well, today the wind got the best of it and blew it backwards. One of the spokes snapped and got caught up in my hair. Then it just collapsed.

I hope it doesn't rain anymore this week or I will be forced to go into one of those upscale boutiques and snag an umbrella out of their umbrella holder. You know, the one they make customers put their umbrellas in so they won't drip water everywhere?

On another note, my brother fixed my car again. I'd like to thank him. I would also like to apologize to the guy I rolled my eyes at yesterday. The rearview mirror fell off of my windshield again, so I pulled over and got out the superglue I keep in the trunk. It fixed my bumper nicely, so hell, it should work on a mirror, right? (I am not joking, I went through a car wash and the owner came running after me when I pulled away—"Miss, here's your bumper!" I was so embarrassed. He said lots of Dodges lose their bumpers, though . . . hmmmm.)

Back to the mirror. I was trying to stick the thing back on there, thinking no one was looking at me. Wrong! I looked up, and this guy was walking past staring into my car. He smiled at me when I looked up. I gave him a look like "What the hell are you looking at" and rolled my eyes. I opened the glove compartment like I was looking for something in it, because I didn't want him to see me gluing the durn rearview back on! Sorry for rolling my eyes. I did that because of my broke insecurities, bro.

I'm so sorry.

*Embarrassed by her poverty, she is,*

*Ang*

---

## MARCH 6

Dear Broke Diary:

Whew, I haven't written in a little while, eh? Sorry. I can't believe I'm graduating this year. So much to do, like making sure I don't fail any classes and, well, getting a full-time postgraduation job. Haven't really done too much on that front yet.

Oh well.

Anyway, graduation is a few months off, so I have something more important I need to address today.

### FREE RESTAURANT FOOD!

Yes, free restaurant food. That's like two steps above free supermarket food. And it's all mine.

You know what that means, right?

Yep, it means a guy actually asked me out on a date.

No, my low self-esteem isn't showing, it's that being asked on a *real* date is *real* rare in these parts. Most of these college guys are dead broke, too.

If a guy asks you to a buffet, it means he's really diggin' you; if he asks you to a restaurant, you must have worked some mojo on him, because he wants to marry you! I'm serious! I got this info from my male friends!

Well, guess what? I got asked out to T.G.I. Friday's! Woohoo! That's right!! Salute me, my broke sisters!

[All around the world, women pause to salute. Women in huts, women digging through trash cans, women toiling in fields.]

Okay, at ease, my sisters. You know I wouldn't be hyping this date up if it had actually gone well. Yeah, I've already been on the date. Yes, of course I'll tell you all about it. You can't laugh at me, though. And you must remember that no matter what I tell you about this date, I still came out on top, 'cause I got the free food.

Got that? Cool. Let's move on.

Last Thursday, Marcus asked me out. Now, I always saw Marcus around campus, but I'd never really spoken to him. Didn't know too much about him. Only thing I knew is that when I lived in the dorm, he used to hang in the TV room a hell of a lot. Seemed like a jolly enough guy. Always had people around him and he smiled a lot.

So, I'm in the TV room of the dorm I lived in freshman year.

A weird thing for me, because 1) I don't live there anymore; 2) I don't like most of the people who hang there—it's a small, family-knit dormitory, so it's not rare to see people who don't live there anymore hanging out; and 3) someone always wants to start some card game I don't know how to play. And the hell if I'm going to study the rules of some card game when I've got a math quiz coming up I haven't studied for yet; until Penn starts giving diplomas for learning spades, I'll pass and study numbers, thank you.

Well, Marcus must be an ace at spades, because like I said, I always see him kicking it in the TV room. And this time I happen to be in there, too. He starts talking to me, ribbing me about how I don't ever say hi to him.

"Miss Angela, are you stuck up? You never speak to me. Why is that?" As he says the last line, his face scrunches up until he gets the furrowed-brow thing going on.

Okay, Marcus, that was kinda corny to call me "miss," but I'll let that one pass. I just have to hear his voice again. Definitely suburban prep-school bred. Very proper.

"Well, you're always in a crowd, and I don't want to interrupt the male-bonding TV-room festivities, you know?"

He smiles. "Well, I say we solve that problem by going out to dinner alone together. You can say hi to me all night without the TV-room boisterousness."

"Oh, you mean the cafeteria? I don't have a meal plan. . . ."

"No, I don't mean the cafeteria. Let's try someplace with a little more ambience. Let's go to T.G.I. Friday's tomorrow. My treat. I want to find out why you're so mean."

Wow! This guy doesn't waste any time. I guess you learn that in prep school. And wait, he's saying I get to be mean *and* get free food? How can I say no? Listen to me say yes:

"T.G.I. Friday's it is. When should I meet you?"

"Meet me at six. In the study room. I'm going to finish up some work there before we go. I look forward to this, Miss Angela."

I leave campus and start dialing Janelle before I even slip my backpack off. I tell her I have a date with Marcus and ask her if she knows anything about him. Thing is, she doesn't know him by name, so I spend five minutes trying to describe him before she realizes who I'm talking about.

"C'mon, Janelle, you know this guy. He's like Brian's complexion . . . preppy . . ."

"Hmm . . ."

"Talks really proper . . ."

"Oh! That guy! He used to hang in the TV room all the time our freshman year?"

"Yeah . . . that's him!"

"Hmmm. I don't know too much about him. He's a mystery man. You have a date with Mystery Man!"

Her words are wading through my brain as I'm walking to the dorm study room to pick him up for our date. *Mystery Man.* I don't even know what year he is. We're seniors. If he was around freshman year, he has to be at least a senior.

I get to the study room. Marcus is writing on the study-room chalkboard. He's adding on to a formula that's already so long it stretches the width of the board. Are you a brainiac mystery man, Mr. Mystery Man? Um, could you acknowledge my presence, Mystery? Hey, Mystery! Yoohoo! Here I am!

His face is so fixated on the chalkboard, he doesn't even so much as nod a hello to me. It's like I didn't even walk in. Wow. Wish I could be that intense when I study.

I almost don't want to tear him from his work, but a girl's got a stomach.

"Hey, Marcus! You sure you want to leave all this to go eat? I mean, if you want we can postpone."

"Miss Angela! Yes, I was caught up in my work! Sometimes I zone out. No, let's go eat."

This "miss" mess is so irritating. But once again, I'll let it slide, 'cause he zones out while doing math. That's cool. Nerdiness is high on my list of admirable traits. Being able to procure food is a close second. This guy is okay by me. Now, let's get this nerdy gravy train choo-chooing.

We hail a cab and head to the restaurant. (Ooh! A cab and not the bus. Cool!)

While we're in the cab, Marcus asks me so much about myself, I don't have a chance to solve any Mystery Man mysteries. I'll pin him down at the table. I'll find out all about him.

As we approach Friday's entrance, a scruffy man holds out a thorny rose and asks Marcus if he'd like "a flower for the lady."

I'm thinking, Please, Marcus, please don't buy a rose from this guy. It's one rose. He stole it from someone's garden. I don't want a stolen rose. . . .

"Yes, I think this lady is very deserving of a rose."

Damn. He just had to let the rose dude hear his suburban accent. You have to be on some serious crack to hawk stolen flowers. I know Rose Dude will rob us when we leave the restaurant. Thanks, Marcus.

Marcus gives the guy a dollar, then puts the rose stem up to his mouth. He opens his mouth, grips the stem in his teeth, Carmen-like, and grins.

Yuck! Did he think that was cute? Marcus, you're losing points. Not only did you let other people see you pay for a stolen, crackhead-handled rose, but now you're gripping it in your mouth and grinning? Excuse me, one of the bulbs in the lighted "Rob Me! I'm Not from Here!" sign on your forehead burned out. Things must be really different in the suburbs.

He takes the rose out of his mouth but doesn't hand it to me. Must have been the look of absolute disgust on my face or something. He opens the door, and we sit ourselves down in the booth.

I start to ask him basic questions about school. Hell, that's our life, what else is there to talk about? Most of my friends can talk about school for hours, but I swear he keeps trying to switch the subject.

"So, Marcus. I know so little about you. What's your major?"

"My parents wanted me to study chemistry. It's been expected that I would enter medical school. I chose otherwise. I won't accept tyranny, even if it is by the ones who raised me! So, what's the last movie you saw?"

Movie? He just skipped from talking about med school to asking my movie preferences? That's a leap. And he keeps doing that with every school question I ask him. Maybe he really doesn't want to talk about school. Maybe he actually has a life outside of school. He obviously has enough money for stolen roses and restaurants; perhaps he has an interesting social life because of his financial status. I'll follow his lead and ask him a non-academic-oriented question.

"What do you like to do when you have free time?"

"Well, I've been known to spend a leisurely Sunday perusing new museum exhibits 'n' shit."

Museum exhibits *'n' shit?*

Hey now. Wait a minute. I may not be up on my upper-middle-class slang, but I know my working-class colloquialisms. That was definitely a graveyard-shift janitorial "'n' shit" hanging off the end of that there museum exhibit sentence. Something's not right, Mr. Upper Crusty.

If the "'n' shit" itself hasn't tipped me off to something foul, the look on his face does. After that "'n' shit" slips out, he looks like he's been struck by lightning. His whole face changes. Pure shock. Like an evil, cursing troll had crawled into his larynx.

Something's not right here. I'm going back to the school questions.

Hey, Marcus, who's the professor for that Cultural Anthropology class you're in?

"Wow! What's that fellow's name? Darn, I can't recall. I guess I should start going to class more often. Haha."

Okay, that was definitely a nervous laugh at the end of that sentence. But then again, I've actually not known one of my professor's names. I missed the first day of class, and it's not like they start each class by saying, "Hi, I'm Professor Bob." I'm going to throw him one more question. This is his last chance to disprove what I'm thinking here.

Marcus, we're in the final round here. If you get this question wrong, you lose it all. . . . Oh wait, hold up, my shrimp skewers are here. I'll shut up until after my belly smiles.

Yum.

Okay, I'm ready.

"Marcus, how many credits are you taking this semester?"

He looks at me like I've asked him the craziest question. I guess it isn't an everyday question, but that's why I asked it. He looks down at his plate and answers me. "Only twelve."

Okay. It's definitely clear now. The Ivy League has its own unique credit system. Most people don't know this. With few exceptions, classes are one credit apiece. The most credits I've ever heard anyone take in one semester is six. So, essentially Marcus is telling me he's taking three semesters of classes in one shot.

Marcus, darling. You're in *academic drag*.

Excuse me as I out you.

"Wow! You're taking twelve classes? Ninety-nine percent of the classes offered at Penn are only one credit. You must be on the real advanced track! I had to get permission to take six credits in one semester!"

You can fool someone not in college into thinking you're in college . . . maybe. But how is he going to try to fool me, knowing I go to the school he's pretending to go to? Stupid. Bold, but stupid.

I've actually heard a story of a brother who sat in on classes at Harvard to better himself and eventually told his story to Yale and got accepted. This is not that guy. Marcus is a faker.

And Marcus is quite quiet, too. We eat the rest of the meal without speaking to each other. I guess he is thinking about the twelve classes he has tomorrow.

I can't wait to get back and spread this one around.

First person I call is Janelle. She drowns my ear in her signature high-pitched laughter.

"I knew there was something about him," she screeches in

between her hoots of laughter. "He was just too, too proper and he always had too much money."

Everything eventually comes full circle, and by some random twist of fate we figured out how he always seemed to have so much money. He worked in a 7-Eleven by my girlfriend Kim's house, and Kim did some snooping and found out he lives with his grandmom.

Well, now it all fits! Of course he was the one buying pizza and Combos all the time.

Take someone who is clocking minimum wage and set them and their whole check (no expenses, 'cause they are living off Grandma) in a college setting, they look like the man.

I wouldn't be so hard on him if he'd just been honest. Be yourself, man. And he was tying up a study room with long, fake formulas. Know how hard it is to get a study room around here 'n' shit?

I've seen Academic Drag around campus twice since our date. He acts like he doesn't see me. I wanna play him out and yell:

"How much for a Slurpee?!!"

real loud, but I kinda feel bad for him.

Soon he'll find another broke, hungry girl to impress with his convenience-store check. Watch your back, broke sisters.

Ang

## MARCH 10

Dear Broke Diary:

I found some really good books on job-hunting at the bookstore today.

Too bad I can't afford any of them until I get a job.

*Love,*

*Angie*

## MARCH 13

Dear Broke Diary:

Yeah! That's right! I'm dead broke and it's Friday! Guess where I'm going. Yes! Later on tonight, I'll be at the fabulous free open-mike poetry reading!! To prepare for this splendid event, I am going to write a poem about the building I find myself in. Hell, ain't nothing better to do while I'm waiting in this long-ass line. Enjoy! Revolution!

STUDENT FINANCIAL SERVICES
Here I am again, Student Financial Services
I hate this place, it makes me nervous
Unsmiling students, long, long lines
Twelve-page forms, late-payment fines
Three-hour class, oh boy I'm beat
Must take a number, like buying lunchmeat
It's my turn, please, lady, be nice
"Hi, here's my I.D., I can't pay the price
Of tuition and I am on Financial Hold
At this rate, I'll graduate at thirty years old.

I know there must be a loan I can take
I have three federals, perhaps one from the state?"
Her reply: "There is one loan left, a PGL"
This loan will put you in interest-rate hell
Penn *Guaranteed* Loan, I doubt I'll get it
Small print says, "Must check the credit"
So lady hath lied, loan *not* guaranteed
Have you no more loans based on need?
Loans for the hungry, loans for the poor
I'm like little Oliver, "Please, sir, give me more!"
Lady not like Twist, did not get joke
Dreams of higher education going up in smoke
She still looks mean and starts to speak,
"Fill out these papers, come back in a week."

Couplet biyatch! What! What!

*Ang*

---

MARCH 16

Dear Broke Diary:

Gotta love these chain café bookstores that let you read the books in the store, right? They're like public libraries minus the homeless people. They are great!

I'm really in love with the Self-help section of the bookstore. So far, I've had two sets of conversations with God and learned why bad things happen to good people. Not bad for free.

I was going to go back today and learn how to make friends and influence people, but this new cute guy started working there and I don't want him to see me spending too much time in that Self-help section. The books on overcoming drug addiction are right next to the step-by-step guides to smiling more, and I'm thinking, why should he take the gamble on whether I'm a heroin addict or just trying to silence my inner critic? I'm sure the girl in the Fitness section looks like less of a risk, you know?

So I'm home today. I'm denying my bookstore run for a cute guy. I guess I can review the notes I took from that financial self-help book. It was, like, a spiritual guide to increasing wealth, and it was sitting right in Self-help, so I had to check it out. I've been praying for some money for a long time now and ain't none came, so maybe I've been saying the wrong prayers. I couldn't wait to see what the book had to say.

I can barely read my own handwriting on these notes I took. I always scrawl real fast because I feel like taking notes is slightly overstepping bookstore policy. Like another customer is going to come up to me and say, "C'mon! Stop that! Isn't it enough they are nice enough to let us read the books for free? Do you really have to take notes, too? You're going to ruin it for everyone! Asshole!"

Actually, if anyone ever said that to someone sitting in the Self-help section, they would have a lot of balls. Now that I think about it, I wish someone would try to chastise me while I'm sitting in the Self-help section taking notes. I'd look up at them, stare them dead in the eye, and reply in a real calm voice, "Here I am trying to learn to control my anger and you just had to come and interrupt me!" Then, for added effect, I'd start twitching and talking to myself.

Oops, I didn't mean to go off-topic. That could be the cause of my poverty, 'cause the first thing I wrote on this napkin was

"Control your thoughts. The mind is powerful. Stop thinking like a poor person. Never think of what you don't have, but what you have, and you will have more. Make a list of what you have." So I'm going to regain control of my mind, stop thinking of terrorizing bookstore patrons, and start thinking of what I have, so I can have more!

All-righty.

I'm really going to try this.

Okay now.

Hmm.

I have . . .

I have . . .

Okay, I'm going to concentrate.

I have . . .

I have . . . two days to pay this electric bill before they shut my lights off!

No! No! No!!

Dammit. Let me try this again. The key to controlling your wealth is controlling your mind.

I have . . . a job interview coming up and no money to buy a suit!!!! Oh my God! How am I going to get money to get this frickin' suit??!!!

Man! I have to slow down. If I can't sit here and think of one tangible thing I have, then I need to put in more time at the Self-help section!

Let's give this one more try. Something *tangible*.

I have . . . a whole mound of ketchup packets in the refrigerator . . . but no meat to put the ketchup on!!

Argh! What is wrong with me? I'm really trying to think here.

I don't want to say the typical things like "I have my health" or "I have good friends who love me." That's so normal. It's easy to say that.

Man, I wish I'd written the whole chapter down on this napkin, because this can't be the whole "I have" lesson. I don't want more bills! I don't want more meatless condiments! This is just depressing me further. And since I can't control my thoughts, I won't accumulate enough wealth so I can buy and read the whole book! Waaaah!

*Ang*

---

MARCH 17

Dear Broke Diary:

After I calmed down yesterday, I decided to go back to the bookstore. I skipped Self-help and went straight to Personal Finance. I was going to get, like, a real nonspiritual personal-finance book. If some of the personal-finance tips are good, I might actually be able to get enough money to buy a book!

I also figured that if the cute dude was there, he'd get to see me outside of the Self-help section. Hell, I'll be in Personal Finance, so he might even think I have money! Yeah, this is a no-lose situation!

Well, now I'm mad.

I dragged my inner child all the way to the bookstore for nothing.

Turns out the regular ol' Personal Finance section is not for broke people. There should actually be a warning sign above the Personal Finance section that says that. Matter of fact, they should charge a cover to get into the Personal Finance section or rope it off or something. Just give a sister some type of visual clue to indicate that part of the bookstore was not meant for moi.

Ever hear that saying "It takes money to make money"? Turns out that's a cliché that's actually true.

Wait, before I get into that, let me tell you how this "no-lose/ I'll just go to the bookstore and scoop a boyfriend and some real money tips" situation starting falling apart even before I got into the bookstore.

Why was Cute Bookstore Dude outside tonguing some girl down? Yes! He was right outside of his place of employment making out with some girl! I am so sure that is not a way to move up to bookstore management. Yech.

Seeing him cleaning that girl's teeth right near the doorway just drained all the cuteness out of him. Well, besides that, I'm not trying to mess with someone who is taken anyway. I've known women who took that route and they went straight from the Self-help section to Outpatient Psychiatry. Do not pass go, do not collect $200. I don't have the money for a shrink, so I'll stick with regular old dysfunctional *single* fellas, thank you!

Anyway, I'm headed for the Personal Finance section. I'm going to be rich! Do I really want a bookstore clerk with no couth? How much would his paperback paycheck contribute to my future household income? I need assets; he's a liability. Yeah! I'm thinking like a rich woman now, baby! I'm controlling my mind!

Cute Bookstore Dude is out of my life, and I'm heading on

up to Personal Finance. I grab five books based on title alone and plop myself down in the café.

After skimming two books, I unplopped myself pretty quickly. I found not one piece of advice I could use in fifteen minutes of dedicated skimming. I did take some notes, not for myself, but to pass them on to you, so you won't waste as much time as I did.

1. *Pay more than the minimum due each month on your credit cards.* Pay off your credit-card bills before you start investing. The money you save in interest will be more return than almost any investment will give.

Yeah! I'd love to pay more than the minimum due on my Visa. That way, more of the cash-advance part would be freed up and I could use that to pay off some of my MasterCard!

2. *Invest some of your money. Some mutual funds take as little as $500 to get started.*

Oh goodie! Only $500? Now where's the chapter on how to successfully rob a grocery store so I can get that much cash together?

3. *Look around your home. Gather up all the things you don't use and have a yard sale! Have your kids help out and make signs.*

Oh boy! If only I had a yard! Guess I'll have to build one. I mean, I'd look pretty stupid setting up a table in front of my apartment building. Not to mention I'd probably be violating some city ordinance or something. Oh look, it also says flea markets will usually let you rent tables for about $20. If only I could have a guarantee that my junk would be someone else's $21 treasure, I'd rent a table! Thing is, I don't know how the market is right now for bottles of dried nail polish and broken floppy disks.

I will however, get working on the having kids part right away. At least that's still free, right?

*Books suck,*

*Ang*

---

## MARCH 20

Dear Broke Diary:

My arms are too short to box with God.

Not like I would ever want to get in a ring with God, so I don't really understand that saying. I mean, how would they bill that fight? "Angela vs. The Creator of the Universe!!!" Who would place their money on me? Even if my arms weren't too short, am I really going to hit God? I can hear my mom screaming from the sideline, "I'm so embarrassed! She hit God!"

I'd look incredulously at my mom. "Mom! You always said my arms were too short!! I believed you!! What am I going to do now??!!!"

A big booming voice would bellow down from the rafters: "ETERNAL DAMNATION!!"

Then the lights would go out or something. I dunno.

"Your arms are too short to box with God" is a downright stupid saying. Who came up with it, anyway? Why did my mom say that to me? Why didn't she just stick with the basics? You know, like "Don't lie. Don't steal." I guess once my brother and I were placed in the "gifted" program at school, my mom realized we needed more complex commandments.

Or it could be that my mom possessed the knowledge I just came into today: My arms really are short. About two inches shorter than the average woman's. I tried on interview suits all effin' day, and on every damn suit, the sleeves stopped at either my knuckles or my fingertips.

I wanted to ask, "Is there a wrist-length suit section I'm not seeing or are my arms really this short compared to all the other women?"

Am I also flawed because I don't understand the whole shoulder-padded suit thing? Why would I want to wear shoulder pads to an interview? So I can intimidate the interviewer because I look like Steroid Girl?

"Gimme this job now before I whup your ass! Don't you see how broad my shoulders are? I've been working out! Grrr!!! Gimme job!"

Who the hell even decided to put shoulder pads in women's business suits? Some guy who was really upset at the women's lib movement, I bet. Saw his wife was starting to go on job interviews, but she always cried she had nothing to wear (since women weren't execs, I guess there wasn't any place for them to go to get an interview suit). One day, she's crying again, and he springs the surprise suit on her.

Wife: Honey! I hate this! I have an interview, but in the midst of all our protests we forgot to fight for a Woman's Career Wear section in Macy's! How will I ever land this job if I'm in a maid's outfit and the male applicants are all in suits? And plus, I burned my bra yesterday and don't have another one to wear to this interview! [She sobs uncontrollably.]

Husband: Here, I made this for you! [He holds out suit with big bulky shoulder pads; wife cries louder when she sees the suit.] What are you crying for, dear? I made this because I love you and want you to do well!

He was lying. He had the shoulder-pad plan all laid out. After a few days of wearing that suit, his wife walked in, kicked off her shoes, and walked barefoot into the kitchen.

Wife: More pancakes, dear? We've run out of bacon, but you'll bring some home next time you go out, right? I'll just fry it up in this pan.

Well, obviously her husband's fashion legacy lives on: Women's business suits have got to be the most uncomfortable pieces of clothing I have ever tried on. All of them felt too heavy and bulky. All of them.

Janelle came with me to the mall today. She was trying on suits for fun. She "loves" suits. They make her feel powerful, she says. I should have left her home.

Maybe I could have appreciated her enthusiasm a wee bit more if I wasn't on such a tight suit budget: My mom only gave me $70 for suit shopping. I'm not ungrateful, I just think dear mom is a little out of touch. I mean, she's a nurse. She wears scrubs every day and has worked at the same hospital for over twenty years. She has not had to step into the Career Wear section in a long, long time.

When she handed me the money, I politely asked if she could spare at least twenty dollars more.

"What kind of suit is going to cost more than seventy dollars, Angela?"

"Um, a blue or black interview suit, Mom."

"I bet we can find a damn good suit at the thrift store for six dollars!"

"Mom, I'm competing with the rich Penn kids for these jobs. They'll have on good suits, and if my suit looks like it's ten years old, the interviewer will think that's how long I've been job hunting! Not exactly a wanted prospect."

I hated asking my mom for extra suit money. Not that she wouldn't give it to me. I know she doesn't have a lot to spare, but something like an interview suit, she'd help with. I mean the purpose of the interview suit is to get me a job so I don't ever have to ask her for money again, right? I'm sure she looked at it as an investment.

A frugal $70 investment, but an investment nonetheless.

Oh yeah, this $70 investment also has to pay for a blouse, a slip, pantyhose, one necklace, and some matching earrings.

The store saleslady reminded me of all that. I'd forgotten.

Hey! Don't women still earn less than men? We should earn more because we have to accessorize. This world is unfair. I thought the tides were turning when it became acceptable in a lot of offices for men to wear an earring. I wanted the "men's accessory trend" to continue. What if they then started wearing pearl necklaces? And heels? And also had to buy a pair of running shoes to wear from the train to the office?

Oh shush. Cuff links don't count. Use a damn safety pin.

We can't use safety pins for earrings and necklaces unless we work at a punk-rock store with a boss named Blade.

There is just no substitute for a good set of pearl earrings with a matching necklace.

Really. I know because that's what the saleslady at the jewelry counter said.

"There is just no substitute for a good set of pearl earrings with a matching necklace."

I mean, she should know. I suppose a good set of pearls got her this department-store job making commission off my pearl purchase, right?

Or maybe people come back to her after they've landed great jobs and thank her for her pearls.

Man, I'm too young to wear pearls. Pearls are for old people, that's why only old ladies are named Pearl.

I dunno, maybe I should take Counter Lady's advice. She looked so wise. She spoke that line to me in such a slow, deliberate style, I believed her pearl knowledge as soon as it fell from her perfectly painted lips. She was one of those refined jewelry-counter ladies. You know, the ones in their midfifties with beautiful, shiny jet-black hair streaked with glimmers of gray, pulled back in a bun. A crisp white blouse, perfectly manicured nails. She obviously knows style. . . .

But wait, she works at an effin' department-store counter!! She can't even afford the pearls she is telling jobless old me to buy. Unless she has a really rich husband and this is her hobby. Her weekend job. Well now, if convincing broke people to buy pearls is her hobby, then I don't like Counter Lady one bit. Taking a weekend job as a hobby, when people like me need those jobs. How much does she really know about corporate job interviews, anyway? Does her husband come home and tell her about all the college kids he didn't hire that day?

Man, I'mma find me a $70 ensemble if I have to steal the blouse. Yeah, once I rip off the security sensor, it'll probably have a huge hole, but I'll be wearing my suit jacket on top of it, so no one will even see the hole.

Yeah. I've made up my mind. I'm going to boost a blouse. I hope God looks out for me. The universe knows the difference between good stealing and bad stealing. I'm stealing this so I can have a job and buy stuff later, you know, instead of stealing it.

Damn, I wish I could just do the "buy it, wear it, try not to sweat in it, return it the next day" move normal women do with stuff they can't afford and are only going to wear once, but I don't even have enough money to buy it.

God, I promise I will never steal again if you let me get away with stealing one blouse from Nordstrom.

All right, let's do this!

Shoplifting for the economy!

*Revolution!*

*Ang*

---

MARCH 21

Dear Broke Diary:

I am such a punk.

I could never be in a gang. Thank goodness I grew up on the East Coast, where we don't really have gangs.

Everything was planned out. I was going to go to Nordstrom, take a nice conservative blouse into the dressing room, rip the sensor off, put it on underneath my shirt, and walk out.

I picked Nordstrom because of their very liberal dressing-room policy. It's *so* inner-city to hand out grimy plastic number tags to folks, so Nordstrom just lets you walk right into their dressing rooms. No checking your bags, nothing. I was shocked the first time I went into one of their dressing rooms unchecked, just like the first time I went to a gas station that lets you pump before you pay. It was like I entered another world. A rich world full of trust. I shall enter that world one day.

But not today. Today I am here to steal.

A pastel-blue blouse catches my eye. I reach out to it, and it gently grabs my hand in return. See, this is upper-class silk. Dominant silk. Aggressive silk. "Take me, Angela." I want silk like this.

Wow, those effin' tinted half-bubble things on the ceiling are scary. I know there are video cameras inside of them. Is a camera on me? Can the Nordstrom Bubble Cam sense fear like night-vision cameras sense heat? Do I look nervous right now?

Damn, I can't just stiffly stand here with a blouse. How long have I been standing here now? C'mon, Ang, get it together. Examine the sleeves, hold it against you in the mirror. Do all the things you'd regularly do if you were planning to try on a blouse. The key is to blend in with the other customers.

I'm in the fitting room. Nervous as hell. It's illegal to have cameras in dressing rooms, right? But I'm sure this is the part of the store where most people try to steal stuff, so I'm sure they have some kind of monitor in here. God, I bet there is a little itty-bitty camera taped to the wall somewhere. I start looking for a minicamera hidden in the wallpaper. Even if there's not one, I bet someone working the security ceiling bubble saw me take this blouse in. The minute I come out without this tender silky blouse, I'll be going down, baby.

Okay, I'm punking out. If I get caught stealing this blouse,

I'll just look like one more criminal. No one will care that I'm stealing with a cause. No one will assume I'm an Ivy League student who just wants to be on level interview ground with my perfectly designer-suited job-hunting counterparts. I'll just be the black girl who got caught stealing in the mall.

Then there is the Mom factor. Should I get caught and Mom finds out, she'll flip. Thing is, she'd find out. These are the suburbs and they still lock people up for theft out here. Plus, Mom still thinks they broadcast regular old shoplifting stories on the evening news, and she'd be worried about everyone she knows learning about the theft.

"Angie! I gave you seventy dollars!!! Why did you have to shoplift? I have blouses, you could have worn one of my blouses!! What will I tell the people at work??"

*Damn.*

This is not worth it. I actually have a future. I just have to figure out a way to afford to dress for it.

*Ang*

---

## MARCH 23

Dear Broke Diary:

"Janelle, you got a blouse I can borrow?"

Sure enough, she did. Turns out Janelle's mom's friend is one of those middle-aged department-store counter ladies. Janelle has an "in" with a real-life counter lady! She got five career blouses so far using Counter Lady's store discount. She never told me this.

What a way to start an interview day. Finding out my closest friend has been keeping secrets. Now I don't even want to go

'Stress'

98

on this interview. I don't want to be an editorial staff assistant. But I'm a liberal-arts major, so I gotta take what I can get. Plus, all of my internships have been in media, so that's the type of job I should apply for, right?

Unless I want to go to grad school and get a degree in something else.

Um, yeah. I think I'll be taking my ass to this interview.

Okay, just one more rant. Who the hell gave me the bright idea to major in something I liked, and why'd I have to like medical anthropology? The only time you see an ad for a medical anthropologist in the paper is when they discover some wholly intact prehistoric man trapped in an alpine glacier. And Career Planning doesn't even subscribe to any alpine-employment journals, so I'd miss the once-every-five-thousand-years opportunity anyway. Right now, there could be a slew of icemen discoveries with people pulling their hair out right now: "Dammit, we need a team of medical anthropologists now! How else are we going to compare our present diet to that of the iceman?" I'd never know. Right now, there's not even a Medical Anthropology section in the Career Planning Center. Oh, but *Finance* gets a whole shelf. Damn math whizzes. Eff them. I'm going to Janelle's house to get a blouse.

I grab one of Janelle's blouses, go home, and throw it on underneath the $59.99 suit I picked up yesterday. (Yeah, I know. I never wrote about that because yesterday sucked. It took six hours to even find suits under $70 and this suit felt so STIFF and ugly when I tried it on, I instantly hated it. I still hate it, it's still stiff, but dammit, who cares if I'm walking like C-3PO? It's a navy suit that cost $59.99.)

I picked up a strand of faux pearls from a street vendor yesterday, and when I got home, I dug deep into my closet to find some hideous faux-pearl-and-cubic-zirconia earrings that I threw in there some time back. Some relative gave 'em to me for my birthday. Never ever thought I'd wear those suckers.

Pantyhose were no problem. The dollar store always has those. My shoes might be a little suspect as they *are* my nightclub heels. Black patent-leather heels with a small silver buckle across the front.

I started freaking out a little about my shoes earlier. "Oh no, they have a silver buckle! Does silver go with pearl? Does black patent leather go with a navy suit? Oh no!"

There I was, flipping out like I had money to buy some new heels should I have found my club heels to be unacceptable. What else could I have put on? My sneakers?

So why even worry about it now?

What I *should* be worried about is not having anything to put my résumé in. "Always bring another copy of your résumé to the interview." Hmmm . . . What do other students use? Oh, those leather folders with the Penn insignia on 'em.

Damn, how do they remember all of these things? How do they learn all of this? I've read all the résumé books in Career Planning and Placement Services! Not one said anything about remembering to bring a leather insignia folder to carry your résumé in. I'd have been saving up for years to get one if I'd known it was that important.

I have got to leave for this interview, so I grab the closest thing to a résumé holder I can find: a hanging file folder from my file cabinet. Yes, a hanging file folder, complete with thin metal hooks on the ends. Perfect for file cabinets. Not for résumés. Perhaps I will have time to break off the metal ends while I am on the bus.

I'm ready to go. Damn, I really hate this extra-long-sleeved cheap shoulder-pad suit, but this is the corporate business suit, so I'll deal with. I suppose I'll soon get used to feeling like a midget football player.

Please don't let anyone stinky sit next to me on the bus, I don't want to go into the interview stinky.

No smellies sat next to me. It was just a plain old regular ride. I did forget all about breaking the metal ends off of the file folder, though. I was too busy rehearsing my canned answers to typical interview questions. I can now recite my greatest weaknesses until I'm blue in the face.

I have never felt as queasy as I did riding the elevator up to the interview floor. Like I'd just eaten two funnel cakes, then hopped on the Super Loop, the Tilt-A-Whirl, and now my friends are pulling me towards the bumper cars. No, please, let me rest before we get on the bumper cars, guys, please! I'm going to throw up and make the bumper floor slippery!

At least I have my trusty shoulder pads. If I get too queasy, I can always rip the foam out of one of 'em and use it as a barf bag.

Okay, there's a lady behind a desk looking at me. I almost forgot where I was. She must be the receptionist.

Put on a smile, Ang.

Speak.

"Hi, I'm Angela Nissel. I'm here for a one P.M. interview."

The receptionist offers a faint smile, then asks me to sign in. "What position are you interviewing for?"

"Editorial staff assistant."

She hands me about ten sheets of stapled paper. "You can go sit with the other applicants. Tell me when you've completed the first two sheets. After that, I'll have to put you on a timer." I look over at the other applicants. Two blue-suited women hunched over pieces of paper.

Okay, so there are other applicants here, and I'm apparently being entered into some sort of form-filling-out race. Timer? No one told me about a timer when they called me to tell me I made this interview. If this is a form-filling-out race, I know I'll win. I knew all those years of dealing with financial aid would pay off somehow. I know how to fill out some forms! Watch out, competition!

I sit down and begin to fill out the forms. Damn, these are easy! Name, address . . . I'm on page two already. I'm on a roll!

Suddenly, the secretary's voice chimes out, "Ms. Nissel? Is this for me?"

I look over to her desk and see her holding my damned beat-up file folder up above her head. Ouch.

Now see, why'd she have to hold it up so high like it's a flag or something? Why couldn't she just walk over and tell me I'd left it?

One of the other two applicants is looking up, too. Damn, her name must be "Ms. Nissel," too.

Of course it's not. She's Ms. Nosy. Put your eyes back on those forms, missy! Mind your business! You'll never get this job if you can't focus on your work, Ms. Nosy!

Let me get this file folder. I can't believe I left it on her desk. Thank goodness I'm not on the timer yet, 'cause that little episode threw me for a loop. I gotta regroup. Okay, where was I?

Oh, contact information for my last five employers. How the hell am I supposed to remember the phone number of the clothing store I worked for part-time during freshman year? I put in a fake number and move on.

Page three is asking for references. I jot down three good ones. My academic adviser, my intern supervisor at *Dateline NBC*, and my boss at the radio station. Can't get better than that. Put me on a timer, I'm ready to go!

I'm on a timer. This timer section sucks. The first page has personal questions. The rest of the pages, I'm checking a three-page article for mistakes, composing a letter to an imaginary company head about recent developments in the pharmaceutical world, and correcting two pages of misspelled words. I mean, *possibly* misspelled words.

Instructions: If the word is misspelled, correct it.

Ummm . . . hello, test maker! Isn't that what spell check is for? This has to be a joke. I don't want to be an editorial staff as-

sistant anymore. I never really did. I'm just going on this interview because everyone else who is graduating is going on interviews. Now, what I really want to do is go home and take this
hot, stiff suit off before I funk it up with any more nervous
sweat. I can't afford to get it dry-cleaned before the next interview. I'll be going to interview after interview with a stiff suit
caked in old sweat. I really want to go home. The thought of
doing this kind of work day after day in a shoulder-pad suit
scares the hell out of me.

I can't just get up and leave, though. I'm going to doodle so
the other applicants think I'm writing. No, I'm going to fill in
the first page of questions so when I hand it to the secretary,
it'll look normal. By the time she flips to page two, I'll be in the
elevator. She can think I'm crazy all she wants once I'm out of
the building.

Okay, eff doodling. If I'm going to play the crazy roll, let's
just go all the way, baby! Let's see here . . .

"What qualifications do you bring to this position? Please
limit your answer to three sentences or less."

"A: I don't want this position. I do have journalism experience, but after working for various media outlets, I realize
sticking microphones into people's faces who don't want to
talk to me isn't appealing at all. Plus, the media gets blamed
for so much nowadays, and the average starting salary in that
field is less than a year's tuition at my college. It's a losing situation all the way around.

"Oops. I went over my sentence allotment. Hopefully, the
editorial assistant you *do* hire can chop it down for me."

I couldn't believe I wrote that. But yes, there it was in ink.
Unerasable.

As soon as I wrote that paragraph, I realized I had to show the exact statement to Janelle or she wouldn't believe me. I also wanted to capture the exact wording for this diary entry. I wrote that same statement down on the page where I was supposed to be composing a letter to CEO Smith. I tried to quietly rip the page out so I could bring it home to show Janelle, but the paper tore out loudly, and the other two applicants reactively glared at me with accusatory faces. Like I was cheating somehow.

Don't worry about me, ladies. I'm out of the race. The timer is all yours!

When I handed the secretary my semicompleted application, I expected her to tell me to sit and wait to be interviewed. Instead, she told me that my test would be scored and I'll be told if I made it to "round two."

Cool. I was outta there. I'd have to wear the same suit to round two anyway. Probably the same blouse. Better that I not make it.

I've decided I don't want an office job where my entire salary goes towards navy blue suits, pantyhose, and "must have" pearls anyway. I'll be just as broke as I am now. Plus, I'll be repaying student loans. So I'll be superbroke. This diary will be like seven hundred pages. Encyclopaedia Broke-tannica.

Probably a whole lot of people won't understand why I did what I did. But I know there are those who will applaud my boldness. Like that homeless lady on the steps of the building across the street. She's probably done that on a questionnaire before.

Besides her, I know there's someone walking around in a blue suit with a leather insignia résumé holder who feels just like me. Let's rise up and fill in crazy answers to stupid application questions all over the world!! Don't be scared! I'll hold your hand!

Psych, I won't hold your hand. That's stupid. I don't know you like that.

I don't know. We'll think of something. Find that fine line between starving artist and office worker. Hmmm, how about day-care-center worker?

I'm not writing about job hunting anymore. It's just plain not fun. I'll find a job. But even if I don't for a while, at least college has taught me how to survive on $10 a week.

Um, I'm sure college has taught me something else worthwhile, but I really can't think of it right now. Hell, they neglected to tell me about the leather engraved-insignia folder, so they get no more kudos from me!

Best wishes to Ms. Nosy and all the people back at that office talking about that crazy girl who applied for a job today.

*Confucius say: She with file-cabinet folder is not truly free,*
*Ang*

P.S. On second thought, let's not rise up. I don't want everyone complaining to me, "I rose up. I took your advice, Ang. Now I'm jobless." Ain't nothing worse than a bunch of broke complaining people.

---

MARCH 28

Dear Broke Diary:
Sometimes it's not the brokeness.
Sometimes it's the boredom.

Then again, Boredom is the bastard baby of Broke. I'm used to Broke living here, but when Boredom comes 'round for those weekend visits, things get a little crazy.

Like, why do I even keep this diary? Broke and Bored. And today, why did I go to the funeral of someone I didn't even know? Broke and Bored made me do it.

Well, Broke, Bored, and my girlfriend Cheryl.

Why does Cheryl always date these crazy wanna-be thug guys, and why didn't I know better than to go on an excursion with her and one of them?

They aren't so much menacing as they are irritating. Like I said, they are wanna-be thugs. Minithugs. Someone bought them the Thug Starter Kit for Christmas and they haven't stopped playing with it yet. They don't really beat people up, they just talk about doing it.

Cheryl is afraid to go to her current thug Jay's grandfather's funeral, because Jay's sister doesn't like her. I dunno what Cheryl expects me to do if someone starts slapboxing her during the service, but she begged me to go and promised no one in the family would mind. (I don't know why I believed her. Obviously, if she's scared of Jay's siblings, she's not really the one to trust for advice on what the family would or wouldn't mind.)

There's food after funerals, right? Oh, I'm sorry. Is it rude for me to think that way? Hey, I didn't know the man, and I'm sure he's in a better place now. Not like everyone else won't be eating afterwards, too. I've been feasting on oatmeal for too long now, and I could use a regular old non-instant meal. I'm sure Grandpa Greg would have wanted it that way.

10:00 A.M.: Cheryl and Jay pick me up and we drive to Jay's

grandmother's house. He calls his grandmother "Nana Nina." She is the widow of Grandpa Greg.

Nana Nina's house is overcrowded. Like, fire-code-violation overcrowded. We walk in the front door and, well, I don't get much past the front door. I literally can't move. A petite older woman in a heavy gray fur coat is pressed against my left side. Her face indicates that she is not a fan of the sardine style we're in. She shouts, "Let's everyone get into the cars 'fore these floors cave in."

Since I'm at the door already, I become the official doorman helping all of the older people out of the house. I guess Jay would have helped me, but aiding old ladies with canes might have made him lose his hard edge, nahmean? Real thugs watch old ladies fall.

After my door duties are up, somehow I end up in the second limo, squeezed between Nana Nina and one Aunt Clarissa. Jay and Cheryl were already in the first limo. I feel crazy being in this limo and not knowing anyone, but no one is speaking, so it's like I just blend in with the interior.

Oh, I see why no one is talking. No one wants to inhale this perfume smell too deeply.

Oh boy. I feel sick. Nana Nina Nelson and Aunt Clarissa obviously share the same taste in perfume. I thought I had smelled a saccharine-sweet smell inside the house, but I thought it was because someone was actually baking something.

Nope.

Nana and Auntie have bathed in condensed milk and roses or something. The smell is getting worse by the second. My eyes are starting to tear up and blur. My stomach is starting to turn. If one of them doesn't open the window, I am going to pass out. I feel like I'm being attacked by twenty department-store perfume ladies.

God, please don't let me throw up in this limo.

God is obviously close by (for the funeral and all, I suppose). As soon as I put out my prayer for nonbarfing, I feel a blast of fresh, crisp air hit my nose.

Nana Nina hit the power-window switch. Lovely air. Yum, air. Air Max. US Airways. Air apparent. Air. Thanks, God. Damn damn damn! The limo has stopped. The air isn't coming in as quickly anymore. Run the red light, driver!

Damn, we've been sitting here over a minute. The light must be broken. Please go, Mr. Driver. It's bad enough your limo doesn't have air-conditioning (or maybe it does and you're try-ing not to waste it, 'cause Nana Nina has the window down). In either case, please, let's move. I need air, and, well, I need to get out of this limo before someone starts asking me what I'm doing here.

Finally Nana Nina cries, "What the hell we stopped so long for?"

Wham!

Aunt Clarissa's door flies open like we're getting carjacked!! Everyone gasps.

Oh, it's no carjacker. It's Minithug. And might I add, Minithug Jay looks a little red-eyed and disheveled.

Jay leans across Aunt Clarissa's lap to conference with Nana Nina. "Nana Nina! I got evicted from the limo! He can't evict me from the limo! It's our limo! How is he going to evict me, Nana Nina??!!"

Instead of telling Jay to come over to her window, Nana Nina damn near gives me a lap dance as she strains to hear what Jay is saying. I'd tip her, but she is once again filling my nostrils with that perfume and I'm feeling too light-headed to reach for my coin purse.

"Repeat that again, Jay. You got what, Jay?"

C'mon, Jay. Say it just a little louder for Nana Nina.

"I got *evicted* from the limo, Nana!! How is that driver going to say I can't smoke in my own damn limo?? You can smoke in jail, but not in a limo you paid for? That don't make no sense. I didn't see nothing in the policy about them being able to evict me for smoking!!"

Nana Nina looks like she is finally catching on to what Jay is saying. She sighs heavily and grabs her cane.

"Let me out this limo. I want to find out who evicted my grandson."

Nana Nina gets out of our car and hobbles up to the next limousine. I'm wondering where Cheryl is and if she's caught up in this smoking drama, because, once again, someone might realize *I'm not supposed to be here.* Next thing you know, I'll have a limo-eviction notice.

It doesn't take Nana Nina long to get back. She mutters something about "damn Mary-Wanda taking over that boy's mind. Can't believe he was smoking Mary-Wanda in that man's limo."

Well, damn! I thought this was a nicotine issue! Secondhand-tobacco-smoke type thing! Nope, that minithug was trying to smoke herb on the way to his grandpa's funeral and made his cane-dependent grandmom stick up for him! Cheryl's found a winner this time!

Nana obviously settled the smoke issues, because once she gets in, both limos get rolling again. Wow, I forgot we're leading a gang of cars. We held up a funeral procession because Jay wanted to smoke weed in the limo.

It takes what seems like an eternity to reach the church. As soon as I hop out of the limo, Cheryl is up in my face apologizing, saying she didn't know Jay was that bad, she's so embarrassed, etc. Thing is, Jay walks up in the middle of her rapid apologies, and he seems to think she's apologizing for the conduct of the limo driver.

He cuts her off. "Yeah, man, that dude was tripping out, right? Trying to embarrass me at my granddad's burial. That's cool, though. That's why I got him. I took him for these, Ang!"

He digs into his jacket's inside pocket and produces a corkscrew, a knife, a fork, and a spoon.

Lord, since we're at a church, if you decide I should just die right here because I've seen it all, I understand.

Jay keeps looking at me like he is expecting a pat on the back or a Stolen Limo Silverware medal, so I just blankly return his gaze and offer, "Yeah, you got his ass. Heh."

I kinda hung back after that. I was giving Cheryl the evil eye every time she looked at me. During the funeral. During the repast. I just wanted to go home, plus Jay's sister wasn't even looking at Cheryl, much less planning on jumping her.

Cheryl still hasn't called me, and I thought she would at least call me tonight. Maybe she's busy baking hemp brownies with her new silverware or something.

Oh well,

Minimoney Ang

APRIL 7

Dear Broke Diary:

My friend Dan's parents invited me to their house in D.C. for dinner. Free food! Shoot, I'll travel to a KKK rally wearing a "Farrakhan for President" T-shirt for some free grub!

I got a ride down to D.C. on Saturday, and my friend Rich was supposed to bring me back to Philly with him on Monday morning. He visits his girlfriend every weekend in D.C., so we'd ride back together and I'd hook him up with toll and gas money.

Well, trusty Rich ends up coming back earlier than expected and I'm straight stranded in D.C.

Dan is as broke as I am, so now that Rich has ruined our plan to get me home on $5 in gas and $4 in tolls, we are going crazy trying to find some more money. (No, I couldn't ask Dan's parents for money. How would that look? First time over to their house, eating up all their food, then I ask them for money to get home? "Thanks for the meal! Now give me some dough so I can get back to Philly!" I don't think so.)

So anyway, Dan and I secretly scrape coins out of his mom's couch cushions and head to the Coinstar machine with a mayonnaise jar full of nickels and pennies. We score $17.59. The only way I can afford to get to Philly with $17.59 is Greyhound.

In case you didn't know, Greyhound is on the lowest rung of the travel evolutionary ladder. Broke people from all walks of life go Greyhound. Broke college students catch Greyhound. People who just got released from jail take Greyhound. Amtrak is reserved for the rich.

I gotta get back to Philly by Monday at 10:00 A.M. That's

when my first class meets. Dan calls the Greyhound line and learns that the next bus leaves at 7:30 A.M. It's 6:40 A.M. We have plenty of time to make it.

Got to the station at 7:10. We're doing the "Angie made her bus" happy dance until we walk into the station. The ticket line is fifty deep and there is one saleswoman. Of course, it's 7:27 when we're next in line and the woman in front of us is asking the cashier everything from "Does the bus have a clean toilet?" to "Do you think I'd look better as a blonde?"

I miraculously get a ticket for the 7:30 A.M. (Whew! Thank you, God!) I get on the bus. There are two seats for me to choose from. Sit next to the guy smelling like ginseng and liquid Tylenol or the woman who has all of her bags sprawled out on the seat next to her. I pick her.

She gets to grunting about having to move her bags. Whatever, man. Just git yo' shit.

We're on the road at a tardy 8:10 A.M. Ms. Bags falls asleep and positions herself so her hips are damn near in my lap! I'm trying to shift around to ease her off me gently. She won't budge. I'm afraid she'll think I'm trying to pick her pocket, so I just let her sprawl all over me. (Catch me next month on trash TV: "I Had My First Lesbian Experience on a Coach Bus.") I soon fall asleep as well. I mean, the woman was rude, but she was a comfortable pillow!

I wake up as the bus stops moving. I think we're home. Noooooooooo! This is the po' folks bus—Greyhound! We're at a rest stop!

The bus driver stands up and faces the passengers. "Hi, everyone, I'm Operator Thompson. I'm not going to lie to y'all, this is only my second time driving into Philadelphia and I'm pretty nervous. I'm not sure how to get to the terminal. So we're going to take this unscheduled stop so I can smoke a cigarette and calm down a little."

No, he didn't.

Well, I'll be damned. He did.

People get off the bus and come back with Popeyes Chicken. Fifteen minutes pass. Operator Camel Light gets back on board and does a head count:

"Is anybody missing someone who was sitting next to them?"

Silence. We pull off.

Three minutes later we hear, "My husband's not here!"

Groans fill up the bus. Ms. Bags sucks her teeth and shifts her hips away from my lap. Someone in the back yells, "Man, why you ain't say anything before we pulled off?"

Husbandless Chick replies that she was asleep.

We go back to the rest stop and there's her husband, sitting on the steps of the Maryland rest stop with a bucket of chicken in his arms, looking like a sad, lost puppy. When he sees our bus, he gets a big-cheese grin and runs to the door. Several breaded fried chicken pieces flow in the breeze behind him.

He runs and trips up the bus stairs.

Operator Camel Light barks: "Your wife almost let us leave you!"

Not flinching, the man says, "Yeah, she did that on our last trip, too."

*Damn.*

I'm trying to get back to sleep, but the guy in the seat behind me is talking loudly about the medicinal properties of marijuana. Why won't he shut up?!! He is trying to mack on the girl sitting next to him. You know you're on "broke bus" when a guy is attempting to hit on a girl by telling her where she can buy the best marijuana in the city.

I finally fall asleep and am awakened by a tap on my shoulder. It's Weedboy.

"You want some chicken, shorty?"

Now, broke people don't like for people to act like they're better than them. You have to be really careful how you turn down a broke person's offer.

"Naw, I'm okay, thanks, though," I reply.

I feign sleep. But then,

*Tap.*

*Tap.*

*Tap.*

"If you don't like chicken, I got a biscuit here."

"No, really . . . I'm all right."

He starts whispering to the girl next to him. I can't make out what he is saying, and I think he likes it that way. I know he's talking about me. Like, I think I'm too good for his chicken or something. Don't ever think someone mumbling isn't talking about you. They are. If you think they are, they are. We broke people have nothing better to do than talk about people.

I go to sleep. Eff a Weedboy and his gossipy self.

I wake up and see the Philly skyline! Woohoo! But did you forget? Operator Camel Light doesn't know how to get to the terminal!!! He turns on the bus intercom, and his pleas for assistance fill the overhead speakers.

"Yes, ladies and gentlemen, I need a guide to the station. I need to find the Broad Street exit."

Of course the only volunteer is Weedboy!

Weedboy insists he knows the exit we should get off. There are two Broad Street exits in Philly. One is on I-95. One is on Route 676. We are supposed to get off on the Route 676 exit. I know that. And from the looks on other people's faces, I can tell they know Weedboy is directing the driver incorrectly.

Why doesn't anyone say anything? We're scared of him! Better to take the scenic route than have Weedboy mad at you!

Finally, after the driver maneuvers the huge Greyhound bus through housing projects and supermarket parking lots trying to find our way home, this other cat on the bus (we'll call him Broke Scholar Boy), who has been happily reading his *Time* magazine up until now, feels he has to take on Weedboy and get us home safely. "I think we should just get back to 676 and—"

Weedboy interrupts in a fury, "Did the driver ask you?!! I thought he asked me and I know where I'm going. . . ."

Oh, Scholar Boy, I feel your pain. But you must learn the ways of the broke. I must repossess your Broke Card. Go directly to suburbs, do not pass go, do not collect your monthly food-stamp allotment.

So, yeah, we finally get to the terminal.

Over an hour late.

As soon as I see Operator Camel Light shift the bus into park, I push Ms. Bags' hips off of my stomach and jog to the El train.

Thanks for choosing Greyhound, blah blah blah. I have never been so happy to get on the El train in my life.

Grrrrr . . . (*eyhound*),

Ang

APRIL 18

Dear Broke Diary:

Today was a gorgeous day of frugal environmental fun. Yes, today was the day Janelle and I set off on a free guided nature walk.

We didn't even know Philly had nature, but we followed the directions in the free weekly paper ad and found ourselves down by the airport looking at real marshland.

Our tall, chiseled-faced tour guide looked and sounded just like someone you would call Ranger Rick. He was so enthusiastic and smiley, I was waiting for the public-service announcement symbol to pop up and Smokey Bear to join him in putting out a forest fire.

It was kind of depressing at one point, though. There were numerous signs in the park warning visitors not to eat any fish they might catch and not to sit in the grass because it might be sprayed with certain chemicals. The airport is right near the wildlife preserve and the sounds of takeoff were deafening. I felt bad for the animals. We ruined their land. I didn't feel bad for any particular animals, because the ones listed on the signs the ranger was pointing out, I didn't see. I saw pigeons and three rats.

Where were the other animals? What if the osprey, rabbits, and trout decided they were fed up with humans and were waiting around the corner so they could whip our tour-taking asses?

My concern for the emotional stability of the abused wildlife came to an abrupt halt when Janelle ripped open a Big Grab of Doritos. Right in the middle of the lecture, she started smacking on the chips. Loudly. If the animals did decide to attack, she'd be the first one getting bum-rushed.

Fellow nature walkers threw her dirty looks. She was *so* loud. And right in the middle of the lecture about how "modern convenience is paving the path of natural-resource destruction." I dunno, even trail mix and bottled water would have been better. But she had to start smacking on Doritos.

I shot her a look. She mouthed back, "I'm hungry!" I decided to let it go, and if anyone said anything to her I'd just call him out on his own hypocrisy. I'd ask him if he carpooled to the preserve this morning. Then I'd eat a Dorito, too. 'Cause I am kinda hungry from all this walking.

Finally, the tour guide stopped hiking.

"Well, here we are. I'm glad everyone has on waterproof boots." He then took off his backpack and pulled out a box of garbage bags. "Everyone grab a bag and we'll begin the lake cleanup."

Yuck!! Lake cleanup? That's why the ad said "wear waterproof boots"? I thought it was because we'd be walking through some mud. Mud is cool. Wading in a lake with multiple neon signs warning against even *looking* at the fish contained therein is not! See, 90 percent of this free-event stuff be leaving information out of their ads to get you to come.

Why should I clean the lake? Make the companies who pollute it clean it! Who is going to clean *me* after I come out of the lake?

Really, I don't understand the point of cleaning the lake. Those fish are already effed. I doubt they will suddenly become suitable for consumption if I pick up some cans. Stupid futile gesture, I say. Plus, maybe they like being messed up. Maybe they don't want to become someone's dinner. Maybe they like not worrying about some yellow-jacketed fisherman guy scooping them up to put in frozen entrée boxes that will probably get dumped back in this same lake postconsumption. Poor living fish pointing to the breaded fillets on the submerged box, yelling, "They used to be my friends!"

But I didn't voice any lake-cleaning objections out loud. I just grabbed a bag and some thick rubber gloves and followed instructions. We picked up debris caught in the bushes around the lake. We didn't have to get into the polluted water. What do we look like? Fish?

All in all, I'd give free nature walks a B–.

And that concludes our "Broke Review Series." Yes, I know I never reviewed anything else, but I have to go. Graduation time is near and soon I won't be broke! Woohoo!

*Ang*

---

MAY 3

Dear Broke Diary:

Can I get a witness? (Preferably a cheap one . . .)

Did the church thing today. Since Ms. Harriet (a family friend) was forcing me to go, I persuaded my longtime girlfriend Michelle (you may remember her from such entries as "Oh, my O!") to accompany me.

Favors are almost as good as money when it comes to bribing, um . . . I mean persuading friends to accompany you on less-than-enjoyable excursions. All it took was a reminder of the time I took her scrawny cat in while she went on vacation.

Her cat went into heat (get your cats fixed, people!) and was hollering at the top of her lungs every night.

I'd leave the apartment to go to class in the morning and there'd be five thuggish tomcats looking up at me like "When you gonna let the hot little gray kitten outside?" I was sho' nuff running a kitten escort service for a few days. Doesn't pay well, though, so on to my church story.

We pick Michelle up and Ms. Harriet goes waxing poetic about how nice it is to see young people back in the church, blah blah blah. She tells us that there is a poetry recital and dinner following the revival. Michelle and I give each other the "free food" secret handshake and all is well.

Okay, all is as well as it could be sitting in a busted car that looks like the inside of a disco 'cause Ms. Harriet's sequined hat is casting colorful collages all up and down the car's interior.

Party over here.

(Yeah, whatever.)

We pull up to the church. Oh joy.

It's one of those storefront churches that ain't quite made the transformation from store to church yet. Looks like someone tried to use Wite-Out to cover the old "Chinese Food" sign and wrote "Second Philadelphia Holiness Pentecostal/Baptist with a Slight Touch of Mormon Church of God."

Okay, that may not have been the real name. But it was one *loooooong* name. Perhaps this is just a Philly phenomenon, but our churches have lengthy names. Having lived in the City of Brotherly Love all my life, I have developed the Four Rules of Churchdom:

*Rule* 1: The length of the name directly correlates to how long the service is.

*Rule* 2: If the church has no air conditioner and it is above ninety degrees outside, multiply regular length of church time by two.

*Rule* 3: Those little fans made out of large wooden Popsicle sticks with the pictures of the pastor emeritus on them don't do a durn thing.

*Rule* 4: Don't even try to get up and leave, even if you're heat-stroked or developing hives. Whatever speaker is on the pulpit will embarrass you with some derivation of the sentence "If you can't take the heat—get out the Lord's kitchen!!!" The congregation will turn around, look at your sinful behind meekly shuffling out their door, and say things like "Well" and "Amen."

We walk in—of course it is steaming!!!! Either they don't have A.C., or today is the day the devil has decided to bring his flock in from hell for redemption. We're a little late, so we have to stand in the lobby until a break in the service. I'm reading the announcements of the upcoming lectures. One in particular catches my eye:

Crisis: Why Are So Many of Our Men Turning to Islam and Judo?

Dear God, is this my life or am I stuck in the plot of a really bad sitcom? I'm trying so hard not to laugh, but I keep having visions of young men leaving church in droves to worship their martial-arts instructors.

It's like my brain is teasing me. "You know you wanna laugh, Angie . . . go ahead . . . just start with a giggle . . . let it out."

Giggle.

Snicker. Chuckle.

Uh-oh. Quelched squealing!! Rumble!! Hahahahaha!!! Unrestrained snorting laughter!

Pinch!

Pinch? Ow! Where'd that come from? I'm a little old to get pinched!

Ms. Harriet gives me the evil eye as we enter the sanctuary.

Anyway, the service wasn't actually that bad once we got into it. Most people were really happy to see two new young faces in church. We did get caught by a couple of haters who could sense we were there by force and just staying to get a plate of free food.

Here are the highlights:

Gospel choir (or more aptly, gospel duet): two people. A four-foot-tall man and a six-foot-plus young woman.

Everyone in the pews is up singing and clapping. Michelle and I don't know any of the hymns. The woman looks straight at us and sings a freestyle verse called "Nobody Is Too Cute to Praise the Lord." (I really wasn't trying to be cute!!! I didn't know the song!!! Mean Gospel Lady, you!)

Reverend: Good speaker, although he got his degree at the Jesse Jackson School of Rhyme. He also looks right at Michelle and me during various parts of his sermon. I'm not joking. He looked dead at my two-girl crew and said:

Young girls drink gin and juice
While they re-pro-duce . . .
It's called immaculate conception . . .
Not immaculate contra-ception . . .

Excuse me, could you hand me a stick fan? Just got a li'l hotter in here.

All's well that ends well. It was all worth it for the corn bread (yum!) and other fine fixings at the conclusion of the service.

When we get to the car, Ms. Harriet tells me that one of the younger deacons was asking about me and she wants to hook us up. She's listing all of his virtues: "no kids, good job, raises prizewinning chickens . . ."

Did she just say "prizewinning chickens"? Yep, she did.

Where in the middle of South Philly is this guy raising blue-ribbon chickens and why would I want to meet him?

Oh well, the introduction is scheduled for next week.

*Pray for me,*

*Ang*

---

## MAY 5

Dear Broke Diary:

I am thirsty.

Usually, I don't mess with Philly tap water. It has this weird soy sauce/metallic aftertaste.

But I am thirsty.

Last summer, they had official radio announcements telling people with weak immune systems not to drink Philly tap water. My immune system is cool, I get an average amount of colds, but I am kinda scared of water that has to come with any kind of warning label. It's frickin' water!! Everyone should be able to drink water!! Not just people who have time to do a T-cell count!!

I am still thirsty.

I wish I could afford some more bottled water. The weather is heating up, and I've already consumed my weekly budgeted allotment. My bottled water is gone. I don't even have a dollar for a single-serving bottle.

Must quench thirst.

I am going to say a prayer before I turn on the spigot. A prayer for clear water. My tap water sometimes runs brown before it turns clear. If it comes out clear on the first try, I will drink it.

I'll be back. I'm going to the kitchen sink to try and solve the thirst problem.

*Damn.*

My water had a deep tan.

Yuck. I wonder what makes it do that? The pipes? Does my water have a rust infection?

Rusty. Still thirsty.

I'll call my mom.

She's not home.

I will stay thirsty for a little while.

Man, I'd rather my water be any color other than brown. It could be hot effin' pink and I'd drink it right now. I'd just pretend it was Kool-Aid. It's that brown thing, man. I mean, yeah, the brown tinge could be rust, but being as how the sink is a close cousin of the toilet, I also could be taste-testing my next-door neighbor's shit.

And I don't like my neighbors quite that much.

*Parched,*

*Angie*

---

MAY 8

Dear Broke Diary:

First, I'd like to send a shout-out to my little brother, who is letting me use his car in the evenings. I love his car. Unlike mine, it always starts. As long as I remember to put air in the tires every other night (the broke solution to slow air leaks), I'm rollin'!

He doesn't need the car after 3:00 P.M. because he works at an after-school program for high school students.

I'm amazed he is still speaking to me after how my brokeness affected him.

My brokeness almost cost my baby bro his job:

I pick him up from work on Thursday. He looks very upset.

Oh, J.R., what ails you?

He gets into the car and cries out, "Angie!!! You're a freak!! Where did you get this tape from???" He holds up the videotape I purchased for him the day before.

Uh-oh.

Let me rewind for y'all. . . .

My brother calls me and says the program needs videotapes the teenagers can watch when it rains and outdoor activities are canceled.

He asks me to pick up *Crocodile Dundee* (my brother loves this movie but he accidentally taped over his copy) and *Friday* (with Ice Cube).

He says he'll give me the money back when I pick him up.

"Well, how much is your job letting you spend on tapes?" I asked. My mind is pondering ways to make a profit off this.

"Fifty dollars . . ."

"Fifty?!!" I exclaim. "We can get the tapes for about five dollars each . . ."

I hate to see people waste money. I head to the neighborhood bootleg-videotape man!

Before everyone starts yelling at me about how horribly wrong it is to buy bootlegged tapes, let me explain something to you:

Bootleg Man is a poor person's friend. How many Blockbusters do you see in the 'hood or near trailer parks? Hardly any. They usually want a frickin' credit card to open an account. If you are barely keeping your lights on, Visa definitely ain't receive the minimum payment that month!

"Credit schmedit" is Bootleg Man's motto. He even manages to get copies of movies that just came out in the theater! Go, Bootleg Man!

Back to my brother and me in the present:

"First off, sis, did you even look at these tapes?" J.R. inquires of me.

I get totally defensive. "Of course not, Bootleg Man never steered us wrong!"

"Ah, Bootleg Man, that explains it. Well, he almost steered my butt into getting fired. That copy of *Friday* . . . it was more like *Sunday* or *Wednesday*. Looks like some guy was sitting in the back of the theater recording it off of the screen. All throughout the movie you hear people saying, 'Yo, pass the popcorn' and 'Dag, you ain't gon' share your Mike and Ikes?' "

*Oops.*

He continues, "And this . . ."

He holds up the tape in his hand and pulls it out of the box.

"Read this, Ang."

I look at the tape. Oh damn!!!!! It says *Crocodile Undees*.

"Yes, my beloved sister . . . that's right. *Crocodile Undees*, as in panties, boxers, and draws."

I gulp.

He goes on. "I popped it in the VCR in front of a group of teens. All of a sudden a man wearing reptilian underwear is asking a scantily clad woman if she likes it 'Down Under.' Angie, he was *not* talking about Australia."

My bad, for real!!!!!

"Man, J.R., I'm sorry. Bootleg Man is cool. He'll let me exchange it. . . ."

"Naw, um, just be more careful next time. It's all right, I'll return it. . . ."

(*Yeah, right.*)

*Ang*

---

MAY 15

Dear Broke Diary:

If you've been paying attention, you know that Ms. Harriet hooked me up with that deacon who raises prizewinning chickens.

He picked me up on Wednesday night.

He picks me up in an old Pontiac Grand Am. That's cool. Who am I to complain?

But the durn thing has tinted windows and a neon "Honk If You Love the Lord" bumper sticker. I think "Honk If You . . ." bumper stickers should be outlawed. You could cause a collision startling someone with a honk. Why not just wave? Why you gotta be loud about it?

Not only that, but you know how some guys have those horrible silver silhouettes of buxom women on their cars? Brother has a silver silhouette of a chicken.

When we get in the car, I notice he has a picture hanging from the rearview mirror. I turn it around so I can see it closely. Another chicken.

I'm trying to make conversation, so I say semi-enthusiastically, "Oh, is this one of the prizewinning chickens Ms. Harriet was telling me about?"

His face lights up like a 911 switchboard when a black man makes the mistake of walking through the suburbs.

"Hello, 911. What's your emergency?"

I'm stuck in a car with a chicken freak!!!

But I digress.

My one inquiry about his chicken was enough to keep him talking all the way to his house.

His house? Hold up!!!! "Date" means free food in a restaurant, or a movie. I can watch TV at home!

Then my brain kicks in. Angie, do you want to be *seen* with this guy?

As we're pulling in to a parking space, he is still going on and on about the chicken in the picture.

I wipe the cobwebs from my eyes, yawn, and get out of the Colonel Sanders–mobile.

I notice he's talking about the chicken in the past tense, so I figure the chicken is dead.

I ask how the lovely first-place chicken died.

"Abraham got hit by a car. I like to let my chickens run free, can't keep 'em cooped up. You'll meet his brothers and sisters soon enough, though."

Yikes!!!! His chickens run around the house?

He turns the key to enter his home.

I don't see any chickens. But there is a telltale feather on the couch. Oh my, Broke Diary, what have we gotten ourselves into?

He motions for me to sit at the dining-room table. He excuses himself and glides towards the back of the house. Cool! Grub! I hear some clatter in the distance. Soon, my date reemerges with a wire crate full of chickens.

"They take a little while to prepare, so pick which one you want, you fine thing."

Heck naw!!!! He eats his own chickens?? Gross!! I can't look a chicken in the eye and sentence it to death! What type of country mess is that?

No "Guide to Dating" can help with a situation like this. I just start laughing.

"I can't eat one of your chickens. . . . I mean, don't they win prizes and stuff, uh, I don't wanna cut in on your income, uh . . ."

He looks offended. He releases the latch on the cage.

My word! The chickens start scampering around the room, and brother is telling me to look at their legs so I can determine the strongest one.

Two of the chickens start fighting!!! It is just a mess!!!

I don't care if Ms. Harriet is my mom's friend. I'm going to knock her out the next time I see her.

Damn, I want to go home.

Yo, no one better ever say anything about my cat being allowed free rein of my crib. Never.

I'm stunned speechless, so he launches into a long, proud

tirade. "I slaughter my own and I'm saving money! Why won't you eat my chickens?! The chicken you get from the store is the same thing!"

I look at him to see if he's serious.

Oh boy, is he ever!

I tell him since he is "Master of All That Is Poultry," he can pick one for me.

What a broke sis will do for some free food. There oughta be a law.

Since he had to prepare it, I got to watch TV by myself for a while, so it was cool.

And I must admit, the chicken was great!

I dunno if he really killed one of his chickens or if he was just trying to freak me out, but who cares . . . I'll never be seeing his ass again!

But, yo, Broke Diary, let's keep this between you and me, okay?

*Crossing the road,*

*Angie*

---

MAY 17

Dear Broke Diary:

My graduation ceremony is tomorrow.

My mom gave me $50 to get my hair done.

I paid my phone bill with it.

I am now trying to style my hair myself. It's not working.

I'll straighten one part only to have it poof up five minutes later. It's like I have my own personal circle of humidity.

I've been at this for two hours now. My hair is going to catch on fire if I touch it with this curling iron anymore.

Know what? I'm not going to worry about the top of my hair. I'm just going to curl the sides. That's the only part that's going to be visible underneath the cap anyway.

Hope my mom doesn't notice.
Feels nice to have a phone again.
*Afro puffs,*
*Angie*

## MAY 18

Dear Broke Diary:

I'm tired. I graduated today.

My mom and brother took me to Red Lobster for a postgraduation surf 'n' turf fest.

Why is Red Lobster considered the pinnacle of fine dining for broke folks everywhere?

Haha. Gotta love my family.

Well, I'm out. I have to find a job. I'm never talking to you again. I'm going to be rich soon.

*Peace!*

*Ang*

## JUNE 22

Dear Broke Diary:

Um, I know I said I wasn't coming back, but I promise, I'll keep it short. I just need to vent. I'm in a broke bad mood.

SEPTA, our public transportation in Philly, is on strike. They have been on strike for like two weeks now.

Broke sis ain't got no cab money,
Broke sis ain't got no car.
Broke sis has only broke friends,
Broke sis, she can't go far.

Ya dig?

Do you know how hard it is to keep up this pavement-pounding job-search thing when you have to walk everywhere?

I had to walk a gazillion blocks today. Around 5:00 P.M., I'm finally nearing home. I was actually in a really smiley, happy mood.

I'm on a type of adrenaline rush from all that walking, and one of my favorite songs is blaring through my headphones. I quicken my pace.

Cute guys in suits are all around me and, hey, I'm cute, too, so I put a little swing in my hips. It's beautiful outside, the trees are beautiful. . . . Goshdarn, it's just a wonderful world!

I'm walking past this outdoor parking lot, and a car that has just pulled out is blocking my sidewalk path in an attempt to merge into traffic. No problem (I'm swift-footed and cute!!!), so without a break in my stride, I walk behind the car. . . . La la la . . .

BAM!!!!!

What was that? You know the automatic arms at parking lots and tollbooths that raise up once you've paid the toll or parking-lot ticket or whatever? The thing chops down on the back of my neck and slams me to the ground!!!!!

The first thing a broke sis thinks of is "lawsuit." But my pride is stronger than money. Plus, I wasn't hurt. Just stunned.

How do I know I wasn't hurt? 'Cause after I heard damn near every person in a one-block radius start to laugh, I ran.

I ran three blocks in under a minute. And I had on heels. Give me my props.

How beautifully embarrassing.

And it's all SEPTA's fault. I would have been on a nice, air-conditioned bus otherwise.

Wonder if I can sue them?

I can't ever walk down that block at 5:00 P.M. again.

*Ang*

---

JULY 27

Dear Broke Diary:

Yeah, I know, I know. I'm not supposed to be here, but can I talk to you for a minute?

I really have to. I'm effing pissed!

Yeah, I have a job and all now, so this isn't even about me. It's about other broke folks. Well, one in particular.

I will never again date a broke college student now that I am a working woman. *Never.*

Okay, check this out. I work at an Internet start-up now, you know? Thing about the Internet is that it never shuts down. It's open 24/7. And those are just about the hours I keep. I have worked almost every weekend since I got this job. My social life is nonexistent. I haven't even worn my black club pants since I graduated.

Know what, though? I like my job and I've accepted the long hours. That's just how things are going to be for a while. I do wish I could go out and party a bit more. Maybe meet a guy and actually go on a date instead of sleeping with this laptop. I have this "underwater scene" screensaver and more than once the bubbling sounds have made me wake up screaming. I thought I was drowning.

Okay, let me stop rambling and get to the good part. Or, rather, the part that has me pissed. End of last month, my girl

Pam convinced me to come to this little get-together at one of her fellow grad student's apartments.

There were about twelve people there and I knew six from my undergrad years, the same people I'd been dying to get away from all throughout school. Didn't like 'em then, don't like 'em now.

They were all going to a club afterwards, but I told them I had work waiting at home and bid everyone good night.

The next week Pam tells me that this guy Terrence from the party has been asking about me constantly. Terrence wants my number, and she wants to know if it's okay for her to give it to him.

Hell yeah! I don't even remember which dude Terrence was, but I'm sure Pam wouldn't hand no scrub off to me! Besides, he's in her grad-school program. How bad could he be?

Okay, so I knew the brother was broke. All grad students are broke. Even if their last name is on every building on campus, a grad student will always give a lowly undergrad that "You think it's bad now . . ." speech. (They always annoyed me with that.)

I don't even care if he's broke. I totally understand. We can just hang out if our initial phone conversations are any good.

He called me the next week; we talked for a good long while. He seemed down-to-earth, cool, and smart. He was in an internship program in D.C. for the summer but would be back in Philly this weekend. He asked if we could meet up.

Sure we could! He gave me his train arrival time and we agreed to "hang out and talk." I'd drive him back to the train station the next morning so he could be on one of the first trains back out. I had to get up for a 9:00 A.M. flight anyway.

He got off easy. A woman who understands being broke who would pick him up, drop him off, and only wanted to hang out and talk. Man, like, did I hand him the gold dating baton or what?

Too bad he dropped it.

9:00 P.M.: I pick him up at the train station. He hops in my Dodge (I got it fixed! Still no rearview mirror, though) and asks if we can stop by his apartment. He couldn't find a subletter, so it's been empty. He wants to pick up his mail.

Fine, no problem.

9:20 P.M.: We get to his place and there's like a minimountain of mail in the foyer. He scoops it up and leads the way to his upstairs apartment.

He opens the door to 3R.

Well, gotdamn!!!

Got-gotdamn!

Gotdamn. Gotdamn. GOTDAMN!

I'm blasted with the most god-awful stench I have ever experienced. His apartment smells like someone has just set off smoke bombs of curdled milk, cat litter, and chitlins.

And this isn't a fleeting funk, like flatulence. You know that stupid fog effect the deejays did at your prom? Well, imagine the fog was curdled-milky-flatulence-scented. That's how heavy in the air this stench is. His apartment has a thick funk fog.

Turns out homeboy didn't think to empty his refrigerator before shuttling off to his D.C. internship. And of course, his electric got shut off for nonpayment, so everything in his fridge is spoiled.

I sit by the nearest open window and thumb through a magazine. I stay pretty silent because it's bad enough I'm breathing the smell, I don't want to taste it also. I'm hoping he'll at least apologize for the smell. It's making my eyes tear up. This is our first "date"; if you're going to make me cry, at least apologize!

But you know what? I'm going to forgive his little dating faux pas. I've been there with the empty-summer-apartment thing. I've just escaped the college brokeness thing. I'm going to let this slide.

Even after he hands me a heavy stack of books and asks me if I can carry them to the car for him, I'm still rooting for him to get his act together.

So far, this date stinks and is asking me and my little Dodge to be his personal moving company, but I'm really not upset. A little perplexed by his impression methods, but I've been in situations where I didn't have anyone to help me move stuff. Helping him pile clothes and books he wants to take back to D.C. in my car is not an ideal first date, but this isn't really a date. We're just "hanging out and talking." The pads of my fingers are now gritty and gray from these boxes, but it's okay.

Let's just get out of this fog and to my place.

11:00 P.M.: I'm searching for a parking spot near my house, when suddenly Terrence perks up and exclaims, "Ooh! You live near Little Pete's Diner! I love Little Pete's!"

He walks into my apartment with me, uses the bathroom, then starts for the doorway again. "Wanna go to Little Pete's?" he asks.

I'm actually not hungry and I still have to pack for this flight. Plus, I have some work to finish up and, well, Terrence is starting to look more and more unattractive to me. I doubt if the sight of him slurping down some greasy-spoon special will make him any more appealing. I pass.

Terrence objects.

"Aw, Little Pete's is the shit! You don't know what you're missing! Well, I'm just going to grab a quick bite there. I'll be back!"

And he leaves.

1:00 A.M.: Two hours have passed since he left. Boy, this must be some meal. I need sleep. I told this guy I have a flight.

My phone rings.

It's Terrence.

"Ang . . . Ang . . . It's Terrence. Just stay on the phone with me. I'm at Nineteenth and Walnut and this guy is trying to rob me. . . ."

"What?!! Someone is trying to rob you and you're on a pay phone? Call the cops, don't call me!"

"No, Angela, he hasn't robbed me yet." Terrence states this like I am in the Remedial Guide to Getting Robbed class. "He just keeps looking at me, so I hopped on the pay phone so I can keep an eye on him. And since he also knows I'm talking to someone, he'll think twice about robbing me. He doesn't know if I'm talking to the cops or what."

What the hell is wrong with this dude? I have to wake up in less than five hours to make this flight and he is around the corner trying to foil a robbery attempt on himself by talking on a pay phone? If this damn fool doesn't get back here so I can go to sleep . . . I love my girl Pam, but she's getting cursed out for this one. I've had enough.

I say, "Hurry up and get robbed or get back here, please!"

And I hang up.

I want to leave his shit on the sidewalk so badly, but even though I'm going to cuss Pam out, she is friends with Terrence and I don't want her to be caught in the middle if someone jacks his stuff or something. If he'd just come in and go to sleep, I'll take him to the train in the morning and never ever have to see him again.

1:20 A.M.: My buzzer rings.

*Finally.*

It's Terrence, with a big, stupid grin slapped across his face. He prances past me and into the hallway. He's just too awake and excited.

"Ang, yo, I am so street-smart. I subverted the robbery attempt!"

To further emphasize his win over crime, he starts doing that dumb-ass uppercut-into-the-air victory move. Then he starts shadowboxing.

"Yeah! I'm street-smart! I'm street-smart!"

It's 1:20 effin' A.M. and Terrence is going on and on. He's "street-smart" this and "street-smart" that.

Rule number one of street smarts: No one who is street-smart ever *announces* they are street-smart. That's only on kids' shows, Terrence.

I mean, he keeps telling about his street smarts like he is waiting for me to go in the kitchen and whip him up a congratulatory Street Smarts Sundae or some shit. GO TO SLEEP, McGruff!

Finally, I think I dozed off in the middle of Crime Dog's solitary victory party, 'cause the next thing I hear is my alarm clock.

5:15 A.M.: I get up to shut off the alarm clock and see that the light is on in the bathroom. Terrence is in the shower. I wonder if he ever went to sleep.

About ten minutes later, the shower stops. I hear him fumbling around in my little bathroom and then I hear the toilet flush.

It flushes again.

And again.

Awww, man! *What is he doing??!!!* Tell me he's not having late-night-at-Little-Pete's digestion problems in my tiny bathroom right before I have to get in there!

I knock on the bathroom door.

"Terrence, I have a flight to catch! I really need to get in there!"

"Okay, I'm coming!"

He comes out fully dressed, chirps hello, and sits down on the couch.

I head right into the bathroom and lock the door behind me.

No.

*Oh no.*

Why is there a lone turd just swirling around in my toilet?

THIS IS IT!!

I rip back the bathroom door and scream out to him, "Terrence, did you leave a turd in my toilet?!!!"

"Yeah, that one just wouldn't flush for some reason."

You nasty ass!! How the hell are you going to go to someone's house for the first time and leave a floater?? I don't care if you have to hurl it out of the window, you never ever leave a floater to greet someone in her own commode first thing in the morning! Nasty!!! "Terrence, man. That's disgusting! I can't believe you did that!! Yo, I think you better catch a cab, because I can't take you to the train station!"

"Aww, you can't just drive me, Ang?"

"No, you *shat* in my toilet and let it sit there! There are plenty of cabs that go by here. I'm sure you'll find one."

And he had the nerve to look upset!!! Turdboy, just go!!! You're so street-smart, take your smart ass out to the street and find a cab!

He left.

I flushed the turd on the first try.

Whew.

Well, you know, I wouldn't even be writing about this if that had been the end of it. Okay, maybe I would, but man, peep this: When I got back from my business trip three days later, there was a message from Terrence on my answering machine.

Turns out he left his sneakers by my closet. Sure enough, there was a pair of seriously used male sneakers lying there. His message went on to let me know he was sending someone by to get the sneakers.

I called Pam and told her to relay the message to him that I was moving in three weeks and if they weren't picked up by then, I'd be chucking his little beat-up bobos.

Three weeks came and went. I'm settled into my new apartment and my phone rings.

"Where's my sneakers?"

I *snap*.

I don't even remember what I said I was so angry, but my friend Tariq was there, so I'll let him fill you in:

Tariq: "Angie said, 'Don't you ever call me again!! You leave a turd in my toilet, keep me up all night with your street smarts. Man, you're crazy!!! I threw your nasty sneakers out! I told you to come get them! Well, they are gone. Don't you ever call me again!! You . . . you . . . you . . . Turdboy!!!' "

Thanks, Tariq.

I do remember the phone ringing again after that conversation. Of course, it was Turdboy.

"Angela, you owe me seventy dollars. Those were Air Max sneakers my cousin bought me. I'll see you in small claims court, baby!"

And he hung up.

I'm fuming!!! This loser is going to sue me for some beat-up sneaks? I don't care how broke I ever was, I'd never sue anyone over some sneaks I left at their house for almost a month!!

If you let them sit at my house for a month, did you really need 'em that bad, Turdboy? And what do you need athletic footwear for, anyway? Not like you're running from criminals!! Just use your old phone-booth tactics, you ol' street-smart Turdboy!

Eff a Turdboy!

Whew.

I feel better now.

But really, was I wrong for throwing out his sneaks? Have I lost touch with the struggling college life? I really don't think so, but I'm asking your opinion.

Whatever.

I hope he does take me to small claims court. I'll gladly embarrass him and relive the whole night on the witness stand. From Funk Fog to Floater.

Even if the judgment is against me, it'll be worth the $70.

Anyway, I won't be dating broke men anymore. Turdboy ruined it for all the good ones.

Just wanted to share that with you.

I gotta go to work now.

You take care, Broke Diary.

Love,

Ang

# *Acknowledgments*

First and always to my mom, my brother, and my entire family: I love you (and thanks for lending me money).

One zillion bear hugs of appreciation to Dr. Alice Kelley. Thanks for keeping me sane during college (and helping me get more loan money).

Love and riches to Ka-msiyara Corbett, Lisa Foreman, Tiffany Hodge, and Uhuru Smith. Thanks for being just as crazy and broke as me.

To my crony, my alter-ego, Aaron McGruder. You've reminded me how marvelous it feels to laugh uncontrollably. You are an angel. Thank you.

Pine nuts and piles of gratitude to Reginald Hudlin. You're a Black Nerd Gospel Choir singer and a genius. You didn't have to do a durn thing for me, but you did (and how!). I will never forget your generosity.

Many thanks to Atiba Adams for saving this book from an NYC death. Thanks to my old-school RMHH crew (sorry the Broke textbook scam didn't work for you, Matt!). To Dr. Deeney, Barbara Cassel, and Valerie Sandillo—I could have never graduated without you three.

To ?uestlove (I never thought I'd get to give you a dedication after all the wonderful ones you've given me!), Shawn, Tank, Dan, and Oracle—thank you for your hard work and understanding. To everyone who knows what it means to be an okay-player—you are the jawn. Hugs to Doug Muir for your friendship and unbelievable brains. To my friends who put their hearts into their art—The Roots, everyone at Motive Records, Common, Dilated Peoples, Talib Kweli, Pharoahe Monch (let's go get a nice-sized salmon salad)—your passions carried over to me. Thank you. Flo Brown, you are beautiful. Your dedication and heart inspire me.

To Harry Allen, Karen Felder, Patrick McElroy, Jason Rodgers, Karen Shatzkin, and all those who go above and beyond.

A big "Woohoo!" to Melody, my editor. I cannot thank you enough. I'm still at a loss for words about this.

As for the other folks at Villard: Ann Godoff, Bruce Tracy, Brian McLendon, Amy Edelman, Joseph Sora, Benjamin Dreyer, Richard Elman, Carole Lowenstein, Dan Rembert, Deborah Aiges, Magee Finn, Andrew Scott, Greg Durham, Allison Heilborn, Tracy Pattison, Libby McGuire—thanks for believing in this broke chick! Woohoo!

Special thanks to LiRon Anderson-Bell for passing Melody the entry that sparked her interest (and you didn't even ask for a cut of the profits!) (smile).

Much love to Femi Guy for coming up with the jacket idea. I love it!

Unlimited megabytes of e-mail smiley faces to everyone who loved and laughed at the diaries when they were just a few typo-filled entries on a personal homepage.

## ABOUT THE AUTHOR

ANGELA NISSEL has a degree in medical anthropology from the University of Pennsylvania even though she used to cut class to learn more about building websites.

She can be reached at www.thebrokediaries.com.

She is no longer broke.